TOEIC®テスト
リスニング・パート攻略

柴田バネッサ/ロバート・ウェスト 共著

南雲堂

The TOEIC test directions are reprinted by permission of Educational Testing Service, the copyright owner. However, the test questions and any other testing information are provided in their entirety by Nan'un-do. No endorsement of this publication by Educational Testing Service or The Chauncey Group International Ltd. should be inferred.

We would like to thank Wesley Lockhart for his invaluable and practical contributions to this book.

まえがき

　短期間で総合的にリスニング力をアップするためには、語彙力、構文理解、プロソディー分析力、集中力、速解力、背景知識の6能力を増強します。

1. **語彙力**　知らない語は聞き取れません。新たに学習した単語は繰り返して音声化し、聞いたら大体の意味がわかるようにしておきましょう。
2. **構文**　今までの得点が450以下の場合は構文・文法理解を速めるためのスラッシュ・リーディングを一週間ほど続けてみましょう。
3. **プロソディー分析力**　プロソディーとはアクセント、イントネーション、リズム、ストレス、ポーズなどの音声要素の総称です。文章を聞いて、これらを分析できるかどうかで英語運用能力に大きな差がつきます。
4. **集中力**　耳で聞きながら同時に話す訓練で通常以上の集中力を養えます。
5. **速解力**　ナチュラル・スピードに慣れる練習を行います。
6. **背景知識**　自分の得意分野の話題は、たとえ単語がわからなくても大体の内容が理解できるはずです。英語力の足りないところは一般常識や知識でカバーするための基礎作りをします。本書はビジネス・シチュエーションを背景にしたビジネス会話の語彙と表現の紹介に的を絞り徹底攻略を目指します。

　本書の第1章では以上の6つの分野に対しての具体的な強化法を説明しています。3ヶ月ほどで効果が見えてくるはずです。
　第2章ではTOEIC試験のリスニングでスコアを伸ばすのに重要なカギとなっているPart IIとPart IIIに焦点をあてます。頻出される設問をパターン化し、応答方法を分析し、練習問題でスコアアップを狙います。リスニングのスコアを上げるためにはPart II & IIIを合わせ、音読練習（Fluent Reading）と、少なくとも200の練習問題を聴いて下さい。
　Part IVの対策としては情報処理速度を上げる練習を行います。知らない語が出てきても気にせずに、全体像をとらえることを目標にしてください。問題文を聞き流すのではなく、復習として音声化することが大切です。

　そして試験の直前には、リスニングの基本問題をもう一度聞きなおすことと、文法の基本である約200のパターンを復習することをお勧めします。

本書の特徴

● スコア別学習法掲載
リスニング力をアップするにはまずウィーク・ポイントを知らなければなりません。通訳訓練で用いられるリスニング力の判断基準を知り，その強化法を紹介します。

● 見開き形式で問題と参考を掲載
本書では基本的に左ページに問題，右ページに対訳と解答を掲載しており，対照しやすくなっています。

● ビジネス・シチュエーションの会話問題に重点
速聴に慣れるための基礎練習となる Part II と Part III の問題に比重を置きました。これらのパートには特に力を入れてください。これらができるかどうかでレベルアップの幅が違ってくると言っても過言ではありません。

● 過去の問題を徹底分析
既出問題をパターン化して，傾向と対策を検討します。既出問題のパターン別出題数に比例した練習問題数になっています。

● 頻出問題，基本問題を明記
過去問題から今後の出題傾向をしぼり，特に出題頻度の高いと思われる問題にはマークが付いています。

第1章
リスニングの強化法　通訳訓練を応用したトレーニング

第2章
基礎語彙の掲載
解答のコツと練習問題

目　次

第1章 リスニング力の強化法　　　7

1. スコア別学習法
2. TOEICの採点の目安
3. リスニング力をアップする基本練習
4. 総合力強化のための学習素材
5. ウィーク・ポイントの分析
6. リスニング力アップのためのトレーニングと効果

第2章 TOEICパート別攻略　　　21

Part I　写真描写問題の攻略法
　解答のコツ 22
　練習問題　20題 30
　解答 40

Part II　応答問題の攻略法
　解答のコツ 48
　練習問題　140題 58
　解答 60

Part III　会話問題の攻略法
　解答のコツ 116
　練習問題　100題 123
　解答 140

Part IV　説明文問題の攻略法
　解答のコツ 208
　練習問題　40題 211
　解答 218

第1章 リスニング力の強化法

1. スコア別学習法
2. TOEICテストの採点目安
3. リスニング力をアップする基本練習
4. 総合力強化のための学習素材
5. ウィーク・ポイントの分析
6. リスニング力アップのためのトレーニングと効果

1．スコア別学習法
－音声練習は語学運用能力アップのカギ－

350点以下の場合
基礎力をつけ中高の教科書を徹底的に音読し，文法を総復習する必要があります。これらの教科書を100回くらいずつ音読しましょう。テキスト暗記するだけでもスコアを500点台にのせることが可能です。認識語彙として4000語の定着を目指します。

470点以下の場合
リスニングとリーディングの得点に100点以上の開きがある場合はウィーク・ポイント対策を練ることから始めます。
リスニング力，語彙力，速読読解力，文法力の5事項の中から一番苦手なものを突き止めてください。誤用指摘問題を練習するだけでランクアップする事も可能です。認識語彙は5000語習得を目指します。

600点以下の場合
教材を時事英語とビジネス英語の実社会に即したものを中心に置き，長文の音読，速読練習に比重を移します。本書で挙げるインターネット素材やCD，テープ，2ヶ国語放送などを活用してください。認識語彙は6000語習得を目指します。

730点以下の場合
文法が弱い場合はPart VとVIの基礎構文である200パターンをもう一度チェックし，ビジネス英語の語彙を強化します。認識語彙を7000語レベルに引き上げる努力をします。ALCのSLV12000語などを利用してください。まず7,000語を基礎単語として瞬時に理解できるように，なるべく音読練習の繰り返しによって語彙数を増やします。

860点以下の場合
頻出パターンをマスターし，1分間に170語以上を黙読できることが条件となります。リスニングが弱点である場合，自分の発音がカタカナ発音になっていないか，ネイティブのリズムやイントネーションを正確に真似できるかなども判断の材料にしてください。認識語彙は8000語習得を目指します。
学習素材はネイティブ対象に制作されたナチュラル・スピードで読まれたニュースや映画などを使用します。

リスニング力の強化法

2. TOEICテストの採点目安

　TOEICはコミュニケーション能力を測定するテストです。実力がつけばつくほどスコアが伸びますし，学習が停滞すると伸びません。点数が30点増減してもそれは誤差の範囲内の変化ですから一喜一憂することではありません。

	Part I	Part II	Part III	Part IV
470点以上をとるための正解数	18	17	8	6
730点以上をとるための正解数	18以上	25	18	10
860点以上をとるための正解数	19以上	28	28	14

● リスニング問題正解数とスコアの目安

正解数	テストスコア	正解数	テストスコア
98以上	495	50	225
95	490	45	195
90	475	40	160
85	450	35	130
80	420	30	100
75	380	25	65
70	345	20	35
65	320	18	25
60	285	16	10
55	255	15～0	5

　平均的な受験者のスコアを調べてみるとリーディングよりリスニングの方の点数が70点ほど高くなっています。ここから単純に考えてみると，ある平均的な受験者が600点をとるにはリスニングの正解率が70～75％である必要があると言えます。

リスニング力の強化法

3. リスニング力をアップする基本練習

> **聴解力トレーニングの4原則**
> 4原則　1. プロソディー分析と音読を毎日実行する。
> 　　　　2. リスニングをする場合は活字に頼らない。
> 　　　　3. 集中して練習する。（精聴）
> 　　　　4. スピードがゆっくり過ぎるものは使用しない。

❶ プロソディー（韻律）分析と区切り聴き

　音読練習をする前にCDを聞きながら，単語の発音はもとより，イントネーション（上がり下がり），強弱，ポーズ，音の脱落，音の変化，リエゾンなどの要素をチェックしてテキストに書き込みます。これをプロソディー分析と言います。特にカタカナの発音で英語を読んでいる人は子音の後ろに余計な音をつけないように気をつけてマークを書きます。

　特に次のような発音をする人にとってプロソディー分析は基本練習になります。

> 英文の全てをカタカナで発音をしており，英語特有のリズムや抑揚がない場合。
>
> | | |
> |---|---|
> | 1. manager, to | [マネージャー][ツー]と日本語で言っている。 |
> | 2. I am　アイ　アム | [m]の発音に[ウ]がついて日本語の[ム]になっている。 |
> | 3. Gate 8　ゲート エイト | [t]の発音に[オ]が付き[ト]になっている。 |
> | 4. in an office　イン アン オフィス | [n]の音が日本語の[ン]の発音になっているためリエゾンが出来ない。 |
> | 5. see, she, sea | 発音の区別がつかない。 |

◆ **区切り聴きのトレーニング法** ◆　スピードのある素材の音声分析をしながら集中力と記憶力を高めます。センテンスごとまたはフレーズごとにCDを止め，聞えたところまでをCDの音声と同じ速さでリピートします。初めはスクリプトを見ながら，慣れてきたら何も見ずに練習を行います。先行の文との関わりを考え，内容を記憶しながら「聞く，口頭練習する」を繰り返します。

◆ プロソディー分析例 ◆

強く読む ´	上がる ↗	ポーズ /
リエゾン ‿	下がる ↘	音が脱落する ( )

日本語にならないように注意するものは○でかこみます。

At‿a pre´ss‿co´nference‿in E´ngland,↗/ mo´vie actor

Mi´ck Fo´ley↗ an(d) his ma´nager Paul Bearer↗

made‿a‿pi´tch fo(r) the fu´ndraising even(t).↘

② スラッシュ・リーディング

　これは長文速読のための練習法です。単純なものですが，効果が大きいために通訳養成トレーニングや大学受験生の学習法としても利用されています。10日くらいで長文の理解がスピードアップしてくるのが感じられます。

◆ トレーニング法 ◆　文章を読みながら意味のまとまりごとにスラッシュ / を書き込み，区切っていくというものです。そして文頭から区切ったところまでの意味を理解し，文末から訳し上げて無駄な時間を費やさないようにします。区切ったところまで理解してから読み進むことに心がけます。

　スラッシュを入れる場所は各自の判断や文章を何回読んでいるかなどによります。TOEICの長文リスニング問題を音読し，そのスピードが1分間に120語以下の場合は文章をなるべく文法的に区切ってください。どうやって区切ってよいのか解らないときは，予めCDやテープを聞き，ネイティブの読み方に従ってスラッシュを書き込みます。文末には // を書いても良いでしょう。知らない単語や表現はスラッシュを書き入れた後で調べます。

　本書ではPart IVの問題文を使用して練習してください。

◆ スラッシュの書き込み例 ◆

As new department heads, / you will find that /
新しい部の長として, / 皆さん方が発見するのは

your duties / will include / meeting production deadlines /
皆さんの義務のなかには / 含まれています / 生産期限に間に合うこと /

and handling personnel problems.
そして人事問題を担当することです。

③ シャドウィング（同時リピート）

音声に対する反応力と集中力を高め，ネイティブのスピードに慣れます。発音やイントネーションの矯正にも利用してください。シャドウィングを毎日15分，3ヶ月続けてリスニングのスコアが100点近く上がったという人もいますから，短期間で効果を上げたい人は30分くらい集中的に練習を行ってください。一般的には3日ほどでTOEICのリスニングの正解率が上がります。

◆ トレーニング法 ◆　CDをかけ，その音声を聞きながら少し遅れて輪唱のようについていくリピート練習です。発音やイントネーションを磨くためには英文が読まれ始めた瞬間にリピートを始めます。　また記憶力のトレーニングとしてはできるだけ（5語くらい）遅れてついていきます。

途中で途切れた場合は，またできるところから始めてください。声を出して練習するのが難しい場合は，唇だけを動かすサイレント・シャドウィングでウォーミングアップしてから徐々に音声練習をしてください。また，初めはスクリプトを見ながら練習をしてもよいですが，最終的には何も見ないで全文がシャドウ（同時リピート）できるようにしてください。上級者は初見から何も見ずにリピートし，うまくいかなかったところだけを集中的に練習します。

④ ディクテーション

シャドウィングと同等の効果が得られます。ディクテーションは総合的な処理能力を測定する学習法です。

◆ トレーニング法 ◆　CDを聞きながら全文を書き取ります。初めは自分のよいと思うところでCDを止め，書いていきます。耳が慣れてきたと感じられたときはワン・センテンスを聞いてからCDを止めるようにします。復習のためには，予め穴埋め問題を作成しておいて練習してもよいでしょう。

⑤ その他　リテンション練習

スコアが860点の上級者は語彙の学習とともに，Part IVの説明文問題で得点を伸ばすことを考えるべきでしょう。30秒から1分30秒くらいの文を聞き，放送の状況を素早くイメージ化し，記号などで表します。その記号を1つ見たらそれに関連した事項を少なくとも3つは思い出すように練習を重ねます。またCDを使ってワンセンテンスごとに口頭訳出することで情報保持の練習ができます。

4．総合力強化のための学習素材

a. ビデオ・映画を利用する

　　TOEICのスコアがCレベル以上の場合，それを着実に高めていくためには弱点を克服していくだけでなく，学習の幅を広げて時事英語を勉強していくのが一番効果的だと言われています。中級以上を目指す人たちが使える英語を身につけるためには，活字に頼らず，視聴覚に訴えるビデオを使用しながら訓練を重ねるのが大切です。教材としてはもちろん，ビデオのスクリプトがあるものがよく，CNNのニュースや英語の字幕がついているニュースも役に立ちます。

　　TOEICはビジネスに重きを置く試験ですから，ネイティブのために書かれた記事を読み聞き，自然なスピードと表現になじんでいく事が重要です。ビデオは難易度に従って見直しの回数を決めてください。

b. 中級・上級者のための語彙のテキスト "Word Up!"（南雲堂）高山英士著
文脈の中で語彙が覚えられるように例文で語彙が紹介されています。

c. THE　NEWS　　株式会社ノトス
　　　　　　　　http://home.att.ne.jp/yellow/notes/contact.htm/
　　最新の時事英語を3通りの方法（ナチュラル・スピード，ポーズ付き，区切り聴き＋日本語訳）で聞き，慣用表現，語彙，背景知識などを学びながら英語運用能力を総合的にアップするように工夫されています。どのレベルにもお勧めですが，初歩の同時通訳練習にも適しています。

d. インターネットの音声素材を利用する

　　インターネットで音声教材を収集する事ができます。ラジオ，テレビ，雑誌の記事を使って最新情報を読み，聞き，ビデオで見たりできます。また，ほとんどの音声記事は無料でダウンロードできるソフト（Real Player）で聞くことができます。いろいろな素材を聞くことによって内容の予測をする力が養成されます。英語力が無くても背景知識があれば解ける問題もありますから，週に一回くらいは次に挙げるのサイトにアクセスしてみるのも上手な勉強法です。

　1. 英語学習の定番サイト
　　　http://www.nifty.ne.jp/forum/fhonyaku/link.htm
　　英字新聞，雑誌，放送局，オンライン辞書などにアクセスするのに便利です。

2. CBS http://www.cbs.com の60minutesのA few minute with Andy Rooney とCNN ラーニング・ソーセス http://www.cnn.literacynet.org/cnnsf/home.html はどの番組をとってもスクリプトとビデオが容易に入手できます。

3. ボイス・オブ・アメリカ http://www.voa.gov/thisweek/ と
http://www.voanews.com/specialenglish/
ボイス・オブ・アメリカのTHIS WEEKもビデオとスクリプトを同時に利用できるので便利です。スピードがあまり速くないものから始めたいときはspecial English を試してください。

4. ホワイトハウス http://www.whitehouse.gov/
アメリカのホワイトハウスにアクセスして大統領のスピーチを入手してください。特に大統領のラジオ・スピーチは毎週更新され、しかも、音声を聴きながら原稿を読みたい人にお勧めです。

5. ラジオ http://www.nhk.or.jp/daily/english/
ラジオ日本のオンラインDaily Newsはだれにでも手軽に利用できるインターネット素材です。このプログラムの良いところは、ニュースのスクリプトがダウンロードできることと、ビデオを見ながらスクリプトを読むことができることです。各記事は簡潔で、5〜6センテンスからなっており、単語の学習にもスピーキング練習の基本パターン増強にも適しています。

6. 語彙 http://www.alc.co.jp/goi/index.html
日常会話を円滑に行うためには3,000語を習得し、リスニング対策としてはこれに4,000語を認識できる単語として補強します。長文問題を読んでまずほとんど知らない語がないようにするにはさらに3,000語を加えます。まずアルク社の標準語彙水準12,000（SVL 12,000）の単語の一覧などを利用して自分の語彙レベルを知ることが第一歩です。

7. その他 http://www.worldvillage.org/lang/radio-tv.htm/
福島県国際交流協会によるサイト。英語学習用の素材紹介。

8. Listening-English.com http://www.listening-english.com
ディレクトリー型のリンク集。生の英語がネットで聞けるので便利です。

5．ウィーク・ポイントの分析

　リスニング・スキルのどこが弱いのか分析してみましょう。リスニングの問題点は大まかには3つあると言えます。次のリストの中に当てはまる事柄があるか調べ，それぞれのトレーニング法を参照してください。

A　語彙に関するウィーク・ポイント分析
1. まったく聞いたことがない単語が多い。
2. 聞いたことがある単語なのに意味がわからない。
3. 音はまったく聞き取れないが，スクリプトを見ると意味がわかる。

B　構文に関するウィーク・ポイント分析
1. 速く読まれると単純な構文が聞き取れない，またはよくわからない。
2. 挿入句，否定疑問，付加疑問が把握できない。長い主語や目的語についてくことができない。複文 although や or などを含んだ長いセンテンスが聞き取れない。

C　音声の聞き取りに関するウィーク・ポイント分析
1. 英語で話されると全然わからない。類似語が聞き取れない。
2. 何も見ずにセンテンスをリピートできるのに，話された意味がわからない。（単語はわかるのに，話された内容の情報処理ができない。）
3. センテンスの区切れがわからない。
4. ゆっくりだとわかる，または繰り返されればわかるのに，ネイティブが自然なスピードで話すとついていけない。選択肢が多いと混乱する。
5. わからない個所が出てくると気になり，集中できなくなる。
6. シャドウィングはできるのに選択問題の正解率が低い。（60％以下）聞いたときはわかったのに後で内容を思い出せない。（情報保持力が必要）

Ⓐ 語彙に関するウィーク・ポイント分析

1. まったく聞いたことがない単語が多い。
中学・高校の英語教科書の基礎単語3000語を覚えなおす必要があります。

◆ **トレーニング法** ◆　中学・高校の英語教科書，またはそれに類するものの音読練習が基本学習法になります。頻出単語を対訳で学習し，発音を調べます。単語だけでなく，短文を覚えると有利です。自分が使える英語のセンテンスを増やしながら取り組んでください。またディクテーション練習も効果が大きいですが，スペリング問題は出題されませんからまずは単語の認識に焦点をあてることが第一です。長文の未知語をまとめて機械翻訳で訳し，これらをまとめて覚えるのも短期間に単語を蓄積したい人には良い方法の一つでしょう。

2. 聞いたことがある単語なのに意味がわからない。
訳語の幅が小さい。1単語に対して1つの意味しか知らない。

◆ **トレーニング法** ◆　TOEICに頻出する重要単語をまとめておくことが必要です。board, union, benefits, allowance, bill, term等の名詞や，fine, draw, blow等のように複数の意味を持つ一見やさしい単語に注意します。単語を知っているのに意味が通じない時は必ず辞書で調べてみる事が鉄則です。これも例文と併せて把握しましょう。

3. 音はまったく聞き取れないが，スクリプトを見ると意味がわかる。
基本はできているのに，「聞く」と「話す」の訓練が不足している。

◆ **トレーニング法** ◆　頭のなかでは日本語を管理する言語野と英語を管理する言語野は違った場所にあります。英語の音声管理中枢（ウェルニケ言語野）を開発する訓練を行ってください。特にシャドウィング練習（後に説明）とディクテーションはリスニング能力を短期間に向上させるということが通訳学会の研究発表で証明されています。時事英語やニュース英語記事を音読しシャドウィングしながら，自分が何割くらいアウトプットできるかを判断します。テープレコーダーを使って大体のアウトプット率を知り，同じ素材を繰り返して練習し完成度を100％にして下さい。

B 構文に関するウィーク・ポイント分析

1. 速く読まれると単純な構文が聞き取れない・よくわからない。

文頭から理解するのに慣れていないことがわかります。アプローチを「読んで学習する」から「耳で聞きながら覚える」に切り換える必要があります。

　　◆ トレーニング法 ◆　　速く読まれても理解できるようになるには，自分も速く音読できるようになるのが最短の方法です。スクリプトを見ながら区切り聞きやシャドウィングの練習をする事から始めてください。またディクテーション練習にはナチュラルスピードで読まれている物を用い，センテンスを聞いてその構成を確認します。

2. 挿入句，否定疑問，付加疑問が把握できない。

長い主語や目的語についていくことができない。
複文（although等を含んだ長いセンテンス）が聞き取れない。

　　◆ トレーニング法 ◆　　文章の構成を復習してください。単語が12語以上及ぶ複文や重文を聞き取れるようになるには，そのような文章に慣れることが必要です。長いセンテンスを読み，次にはその文章を書いてみるのもよい練習法です。
　またパターンごとにまとめて，集中的に練習を行うことも役に立ちます。

C 音声の聞き取りに関するウィーク・ポイント分析

1. 英語で話されると全然わからない。類似語が聞き取れない。

理由の一つは語彙力がないことです。また，日本語化したカタカナ英語で文章を読んでいるため，自然なスピードの英語を聞いた時に頭の中で処理ができないというケースも多々あります。[r]と[l]の発音や母音聞き取りが弱い事が考えられます。run/ran, work/walk, she/see, hat/hut, ear/year の発音は区別できますか。

　　◆ トレーニング法 ◆　　語彙が少なくて聞き取れない初歩の段階の人はTOEICに頻出する単語を中心に認識できる単語を増やす努力が必要です。同時に音声教材を用いての音読練習を3ヶ月間続けて行ってみてください。

第1章 リスニング力の強化法

☆ **プロソディー分析（ネイティブの発音全般を分析）を1ヶ月間続けよう。**

語彙力があっても聞き取りができない人は，音読練習をするときには発音の違いを意識的に区別していく習慣をつけて下さい。特に英語の母音は日本語にない音がありますから，発音記号と音をセットで覚えると聞き取りが楽になるはずです。子音のr/l, s/thはTOEIC Part I, Part IIに頻出の単語を中心に学習して下さい。ネイティブの発音を確認して自分でも発音練習をします。単語だけでなく，苦手な単語を含んでいるセンテンスも練習し，発音し分けることができるように目指して下さい。TOEICのPart Iの練習問題のディクテーションを集中的に行えば音が聞き分けられるようになります。

2. **何も見ずにセンテンスをリピートできるのに，話された意味がわからない。（単語はわかるが，話された内容の情報処理ができない。）**

文法・慣用句などの基本をマスターしていないため内容が正確に把握できないか，リエゾン（音がつながる）や弱く発音される単語（前置詞，冠詞，接続詞など）の聞き取りが弱いなどが原因です。

◆ **トレーニング法** ◆　　as long as, she must have been などはどう読みますか。as /long /as, she/ must/ have/ been と，単語を区切って読んではいませんか。よくセットで使われる語句は一息で，1単語のように読まれます。
　適切な発音をするには自分が聞き取れなかったセンテンスを繰り返し聞き，自分もなるべくネイティブに近い発音をする練習をします。自分が発音できる音は聞き取れます。TOEICのPart IIIまたはPart IV，ニュースのようなスピードが少し速めの音声教材を使用して音声練習をします。

3. **センテンスの区切れ目がわからない。**

自然なスピードの英語を聞く事に慣れていないと推測できます。

◆ **トレーニング法** ◆　　センテンスが完結するときは，大体の場合イントネーションが下がり，一つ情報提供が終わるというシグナルがだされます。それを意識して音声教材を使用しながら音声練習をします。教材を読んでいるネイティブと同じスピードで読めるようになるまで繰り返してください。プロソディー分析はセンテンス完結部がはっきりわかるようになるまで続けます。

リスニング力の強化法

4. **ゆっくりだとわかる・繰り返されればわかるが，ネイティブが自然なスピードで話すとついていけない。選択肢が多いと混乱する。**

文頭から理解ができず，反応が遅いこと，または集中力が弱い。速いスピードについていく耳ができてない。背景知識がない。ビジネス関連事項の学習が不十分であるなどが主な原因です。

　　◆ トレーニング法 ◆　　スクリプトのある長文を用います。まずCDを聞きながらイントネーションや，リエゾンなどを中心にプロソディー分析を行います。特にTOEICのスコアが500点以下の場合は問題集を中心に学習し，500点以上の人は時事英語を補強すると点数の伸びが速くなります。

5. **わからない個所が出てくると気になり，集中できなくなる。**

内容の予測練習と大意をつかむ練習が必要です。文章中の単語が10％わからなくても大体の意味はつかむという心構えを持ってください。

　　◆ トレーニング法 ◆　　わからない個所は聞き飛ばし，内容を予測しながら要旨をつかみとる態度を身に付ける練習をします。TOEICのPart IVを聞き要旨を個条書きにし，それをもとに大意要約の練習をします。何回聞いても同じようにしか聞こえない文章は自分で穴埋め問題を作成し，ディクテーションをします。スクリプトで聞こえなかった所を確認し，発音パターンをインプットしてください。

6. **シャドウィングはできるのに選択問題の正解率が低い。聞いたときはわかったのに後で内容を思い出せない。**

反応が速く音感もよいのですが文頭から理解する速聴速解力が弱いとわかります。聞いたときは理解できたのに後になって内容が思い出せない人は漫然と聞く癖がついています。理解をすることと記憶することは二つの違った技能であると考えて意識的に記憶力トレーニングを行います。

　　◆ トレーニング法 ◆　　音読して全ての意味がわかってから聴解練習を集中的に行います。問題集で学習する場合，選択問題は，まず選択肢を読んでから答え，それができない場合は選択肢に頼らず集中して内容を覚える訓練をします。人によってはメモ取りの練習も効果があります。メモはキイワードのみを，それをもとに内容を30秒くらい暗記する練習をします。Part IVの練習問題を用います。

　通訳者記憶力強化トレーニングで一番有名なものはリテンション練習と呼ばれています。初見で聴いた文章を10秒くらいたってからリピートし，その正確さを確認するものです。短いフレーズから

始め、最終的には5センテンスくらいが再生できるようになることを目標にします。

● リスニング力アップのためのトレーニングと効果

1. 速読スピードのチェック
ホワイト・ハウスのホームページを使用して1分間黙読し、何語読めるかをチェックする。　　（週に1度か2度）

2. プロソディー分析
同上の原稿をダウンロードし、その音声を聞きながらプロソディー分析を行う。（1素材につき1回実行）

3. スラッシュ・リーディング　　少なくとも1回
同上のスクリプトにスラッシュを書き入れる。

4. 未知語・表現の確認
繰り返し出てくるものを確認する。

5. 音読
オリジナルの音声を区切り聴きし、リピートする。
原稿を見ながら、同時リピートする。（少なくとも5回）

6. シャドウィング　　（数回練習）
何も見ないで同時リピートできるように練習する。
（初めから完全にできる必要はありません。）

　　　上記トレーニングを著者の担当するビジネス英語（中級）と通訳のクラスで10週間集中的に練習してみた結果、次のような効果が見られました。通訳学会の染谷泰正先生のリサーチでもこのような結果が得られており、シャドウィング、音読、ディクテーションが聴解力向上の最強の方法であると言っても過言ではありません。

平均アップ率
　　ディクテーションの点数　28％　　（穴埋め問題）
　　要旨の理解度　20％　　（4択問題）
　　音読の速度　25％　　（ホワイト・ハウスのホーム・ページ）
　　音読の正確さ　48％　　（米大統領の演説を初見で音読し、それを録音）
　　著者作成のTOEIC模試Part IIとIIIのスコア　15％

第2章 TOEIC パート別攻略

- Part I　写真描写問題
- Part II　応答問題
- Part III　会話問題
- Part IV　説明文問題

Part I 写真描写問題の攻略法

Ⓐ フォーマット

　　Part I は写真描写問題です。問題数は20です。一つの写真に対して4つの文が読まれ、その中で最も適切に写真の内容を描写しているセンテンスの記号を解答用紙にマークします。このパートは全体で15分ほどかかります。

Ⓑ 問題の提示

　　試験の導入部＋Part I の指示文＋例題と解答例の提示　1分13秒
　　　　　↓
問題開始
Look at the picture marked number 1 in your test book.
　　　　　↓（1秒）
A（2秒）選択肢Aの文
　　　　　↓（1秒）
B（2秒）選択肢Bの文
　　　　　↓（1秒）
C（2秒）選択肢Cの文
　　　　　↓（1秒）
D（2秒）選択肢Dの文
　　　　　↓（5秒）解答用のポーズ
次の問題開始
Look at the picture marked number 2 in your test book.

Ⓒ 解答のコツ

　　集中を散漫にしないためには写真のそばにA, B, C, Dと記号を書き、選択肢を聞いて正解だと確信できるものには○、そうでないものには×、よくわからないものには△の印を書いておきます。

22

D 傾向と対策

写真は17～18枚が人物中心のもので，風景のみや物体のみのものは合わせて2～3枚となっています。

写真は日常的な場面のもので，センテンスはbe動詞やbe動詞＋動詞のingのような基本的なものが90％以上を占め，語彙もTOEICの基礎機能語です。目に見える状況を述べているわけですから「描写の動詞」と「場所を表す前置詞」を中心に学習します。特に中学や高校の教科書に載っているsit, stand, walkなど人の日常の動作を表すものは不規則動詞も含め見直してください。またアメリカは車社会ですから，道路や駐車場，車に関する語彙は必須用語として覚えてください。

問題パターンの分析

試験問題のパターンは大まかに分けて3タイプあります。
1. 類似音の問題
2. 単語の意味そのものを問題としているもの
3. 上記二つの組合せの問題で類似音と単語の意味の知識を試すもの

1．類似音の問題

頻 出 単 語

bored	飽きた	board	板
bridge	橋	ridge	尾根
coffee	コーヒー	copy	コピー
company	会社	accompany	同伴する
duck	アヒル	dock	ドック，ドックに入れる
erase	消す	race	レース
file	ファイルする	pile	積み重ねる
fill	満たす	feel	感じる
map	地図	mop	モップ
message	メッセージ	messenger	メッセンジャー
rail	レール	railing	手摺り
ship	船	sheep	羊
wait	待つ	waiter	ウェイター

第2章 TOEICパート別攻略

2. 単語の意味そのものを問題としているもの

TOEIC 最重要人物

audience	聴衆	chef	シェフ
commuter	通勤者	conductor	車掌，指揮者
customer	顧客	cyclist	サイクリスト
dentist	歯科医	electrician	電気技術者
engineer	エンジニア	manager	マネージャー
mechanic	整備士	passenger	乗客
patient	患者	pedestrian	歩行者
physician	医者	secretary	秘書
spectator	見物人	technician	技術者
veterinarian	獣医	waiter	ウェイター
accountant	会計係	architect	建築家
arbitrator	仲裁人	chemist	化学者
client	依頼人，顧客	competitor	競争者，ライバル
customer	顧客	executive	重役
mailperson	郵便配達人	judge	裁判官
law enforcement officer	警官	lawyer	弁護士
newscaster	ニュースキャスター	participant	参加者
personnel director	人事部長	receptionist	受付係
surgeon	外科医	travel agent	旅行業者

人物・趣味・日用品関係

beard	あごひげ	a piece of music	音楽
fishing rod	釣りざお	jacket	ジャケット，上着
musical instrument	楽器	orchestra	オーケストラ
perform	演奏する	sculpture	彫刻
statue	像	tie	ネクタイ
moustache	口ひげ	travel	旅行
dive	潜る	try on	試着する
swim	泳ぐ	grocery	食料雑貨
a piece of luggage	荷物	furniture	家具
play tennis	テニスをする	paint	描く，ペンキを塗る

monument	記念碑	glasses	眼鏡
couch	長いす，ソファー	cupboard	食器棚
furniture	家具	ladder	梯子(ハシゴ)
satellite dish	パラボラ・アンテナ	stove	コンロ，ガスレンジ
shelf	棚	produce	農産物
mow the lawn	芝生を刈る	wait in line	一列に待つ
walk the dog	犬を散歩させる	water the plant	草木に給水する

仕　事　関　係

be stacked	積み重ねられる	assemble	集まる
cabinet	キャビネット	conference	会議
consult	相談する	copier	複写機
dial	ダイヤル	discuss	討議・検討する
examine	調査する	inventory	目録
mail	郵送する	make a call	電話をかける
plant	プラント，工場	quit	やめる
row	列	stapler	ホチキス
stationery	文房具	supplies	必需品，備品

交　通・背　景

curb	縁石	block	妨害する
be parallel to	平行である	board	搭乗する
congestion	混雑	construction	建設
cross	横切る	curve	カーブ
edge	端	fence	フェンス
fly	飛ぶ	garage	ガレージ
land	着地する	lane	レーン
load	荷積みする	park	駐車する
platform	プラットホーム	pole	棒
ramp	ランプ（高速道路の）	repair	修理する
route	ルート	sailboat	帆船
sidewalk	歩道	tow	牽引する
track	トラック	traffic light	交通信号
wheel	車輪	wreck	破損する，難破する

重要名詞

account	口座, 顧客	accounts payable	支払勘定
antibiotics	抗生物質	appliance	家電
appointment	予約, 指定	architectural firm	建築事務所
audit	監査	automobile dealership	車の販売代理店
awards ceremony	賞セレモニー	bank account	預金口座
benefit	利益 (pl.) 手当	bidding	入札
board	重役会	bond	債権
briefing	状況説明	broken-down car	故障車
budget	予算	bulb	球
capitol	州議事堂	cellular phone	携帯電話
charge	負担	complaint	不平
confidence	信頼	contract	契約
courier service	急使サービス	court	法廷, 宮廷
deadline	最終期限	delay	遅れ
delivery	配達	dispute	論争
donation	寄付	drawer	引出し
efficiency	効率	emergency exit	非常口
enrollment	登録	equipment	設備
express mail	速達	fabric store	布店
facility	設備	faulty wiring	誤配線
feature	特徴	figure	数字
fuel	燃料	fuse	ヒューズ
graduate degree	大学院の学位	grant	助成金
grocery store	食料雑貨店	harbor	港
hard hat	ヘルメット (仕事用)	headquarters	本社, 本部
installation	設置	insurance agency	保険代理店
insurance policy	保険証書	intermission	休憩時間
inventory	在庫, 目録	label	ラベル
legal problem	法律の問題	lounge	ラウンジ
luncheon	昼食会	lumberyard	材木置き場
mechanical problem	機械系統の問題	merchandise	商品
merger	合併	microwave	マイクロ波, 電子レンジ

microscope	顕微鏡	moving company	引越し運送会社
negotiation (s)	交渉	payroll	給料支払簿
pharmacy	薬局	premises	敷地, 構内
premium	保険料	prescription	処方箋, 規定
procedure	手続き	profit	利益
property	物件	proposal	提案
purchase	購入	quota	割当て
quality control	品質管理	raffle	宝くじ
raise	昇給	refund	返金, 返済
registered mail	書留郵便	resource	資源
retail store	小売店	revision	修正, 改訂
seminar	セミナー	shipping	輸送
shuttle	シャトル	stock exchange	証券取引所
stock market	株式市場	stockroom	貯蔵室
strategy	戦略	trade journal	業界誌
unemployment	失業	union	組合
vehicle	乗物	wage	賃金
waiver	権利放棄	warehouse	倉庫
warranty	保証	workshop	作業場, ワークショップ

基 本 頻 出 動 詞

agree	同意する	answer	答える
arrange	手配をする	arrive	到着する
attend	出席する	become	〜になる, 似合う
begin	開始する	boil	沸騰する
bring	持ってくる	buy	買う
calculate	計算する	call	呼ぶ
choose	選ぶ	clean	掃除する
come	来る	compare	比べる
complete	完成する	decline	断わる, 減少する
draw	引く	drink	飲む
enjoy	楽しむ	enter	入る
fall	落ちる	find	見つける
finish	終わる	fold	折る

get	得る	give	与える
go	行く	hand	手渡す
help	助ける	hold	握る
lean on	もたれる	leave	去る
lock	錠をおろす	make	作る
meet	会う	move	動く
need	必要とする	oppose	反対する
order	注文する	pick up	拾う
push	押す	put	置く
ride	乗る	run	走る，動く
scatter	散乱する	sell	売る
set	セットする	shake hands	握手する
sharpen	鋭くする	sign	サインする
sit	座る	sleep	眠る
stand	立つ	stop	止まる
swing	振れる	take	取る
talk	話す	turn	曲がる
type	タイプする	use	使う
walk	歩く	watch	見る
wear	着る	work	働く

第2章 TOEIC パート別攻略

Part I 練習問題 1－20

写真を見ながら，その内容についての4つの英文を聞き，最も的確に描写しているものの記号を塗りつぶしてください。

1
1-02

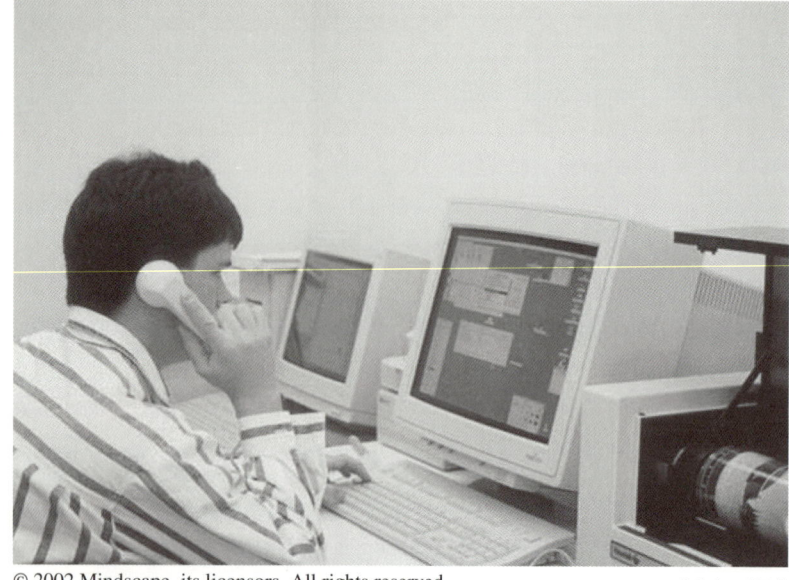

© 2002 Mindscape, its licensors. All rights reserved

(A) (B)
(C) (D)

2
1-03

© 2002 Mindscape, its licensors. All rights reserved

(A) (B)
(C) (D)

3

1-04

(A) (B)
(C) (D)

© 2002 Mindscape, its licensors. All rights reserved

4

1-05

(A) (B)
(C) (D)

© 2002 Mindscape, its licensors. All rights reserved

Part I 写真描写問題 **31**

5
1-06

© 2002 Mindscape, its licensors. All rights reserved

(A) (B)
(C) (D)

6
1-07

(A) (B)
(C) (D)

7

1-08

© 2002 Mindscape, its licensors. All rights reserved.　　(A)　(B)　(C)　(D)

8

1-09

© 2002 Mindscape, its licensors. All rights reserved.　　(A)　(B)　(C)　(D)

Part I　写真描写問題　　33

9

1-10

© 2002 Mindscape, its licensors. All rights reserved

(A) (B) (C) (D)

10

1-11

© 2002 Mindscape, its licensors. All rights reserved

(A) (B) (C) (D)

11

1-12

© 2002 Mindscape, its licensors. All rights reserved.

(A) (B) (C) (D)

12

1-13

© 2002 Mindscape, its licensors. All rights reserved

(A) (B) (C) (D)

Part I 写真描写問題　35

13

1-14

© 2002 Mindscape, its licensors. All rights reserved

(A) (B)
(C) (D)

14

1-15

© 2002 Mindscape, its licensors. All rights reserved

(A) (B)
(C) (D)

15

1-16

(A) (B) (C) (D)

16

1-17

(A) (B) (C) (D)

Part I 写真描写問題   37

17

1-18

© 2002 Mindscape, its licensors. All rights reserved

(A) (B)
(C) (D)

18

1-19

© 2002 Mindscape, its licensors. All rights reserved

(A) (B)
(C) (D)

19

1-20

© 2002 Mindscape, its licensors. All rights reserved

(A) (B)
(C) (D)

20

1-21

© 2002 Mindscape, its licensors. All rights reserved

(A) (B)
(C) (D)

Part I 写真描写問題 **39**

Part I Scripts

1.

a. The men are talking on the phone.
b. He is looking at the monitor.
c. The man is installing the computer.
d. He's wearing a short sleeved shirt.

2.

a. The girl is feeding the birds.
b. All the birds are white.
c. The bird is eating out of her hand.
d. She is rolling up her sleeves.

3.

a. She is standing in front of the boxes.
b. The woman is holding a cage.
c. The assembly line has stopped.
d. She is packing the box.

4.

a. The woman is writing a program.
b. The woman is at a casino.
c. She is fixing the vending machine.
d. The woman is entering her ATM code.

5.

a. The front desk is busy.
b. He is checking the plans.
c. The man is using a lap top.
d. There is a plant behind the man.

スクリプト 訳

1. **b**
a. 男性たちは電話で話しています。
b. 彼はモニターを見ています。
c. 男性はコンピュータを設置しています。
d. 彼は半袖のシャツを着ています。

> 参考
> hung up 電話を切る」
> install 据え付ける，設置する

2. **c**
a. 少女は鳥にえさをやっています。
b. 彼女はペットを買ったところです。
c. 鳥は彼女の手からえさを食べています。
d. 彼女は袖をまくりあげています。

> 参考
> feed えさ
> birdの複数形 birds が聞きとれるかがポイント。
> roll up one's sleeves 袖をまくり上げる

3. **d**
a. 彼女は箱の前に立っています。
b. 女性は檻を持っています。
c. 組立てラインが止まりました。
d. 彼女は箱を詰めています。

> 参考 この女性がどこに立っているのか注目。
> cage 檻
> pack 詰める，梱包する
> pack a case with 〜 ケースに〜を詰める

4. **d**
a. 女性はプログラムを書いています。
b. 女性はカジノにいます。
c. 彼女は自動販売機を修理しています。
d. 女性はATMのコードを入力しています。

> 参考 海外で見うけられるATMの型を知っていると有利。
> vending machine 自動販売機
> ATM=automatic teller machine 現金自動預入支払機

5. **d**
a. フロント・デスクは忙しいです。
b. 彼はプランをチェックしています。
c. 男性は計算機を使っています。
d. 男性のうしろに植物があります。

> 参考
> plan, plant, front の発音聞き取りがポイントです。
> plant 植物，工場，(動詞) 植える

Part I 写真描写問題

6.

a. The pedestrians are walking hand in hand.
b. The sidewalk is congested.
c. The man is carrying the child.
d. The child is clinging to his mother.

7.

a. The people are in front of the car.
b. The racecar is very fast.
c. The car is about to park on the street.
d. He's opening the door.

8.

a. The passengers are boarding the ship.
b. There is a sheep in the pasture.
c. The riders are next to the sheep.
d. There are tall trees in the foreground.

9.

a. The house has three chimneys.
b. Many windows need repair.
c. The house is for sale.
d. There is a sign next to the driveway.

10.

a. The roadway is congested.
b. He likes to play bridge.
c. There are no cars at the tollbooth.
d. The bridge is quite long.

6.

a. 歩行者たちは手をつないで歩いています。
b. 歩道は混み合っています。
c. 男性は子供を抱いています。
d. 子供はお母さんにしがみついています。

参考
pedestrain 歩行者
congested 混んでいる
cling to ～ ～にしがみつく

c

7.

a. 人々は車の前にいる。
b. レースカーは非常に速い。
c. 車は通りに駐車するところだ。
d. 彼はドアを開けている。

参考 群集と車と中心的人物の三部構成問題。前面の人物に関することは予測できるはず。bは状況を描写していないので解答にはなりえない。

d

8.

a. 乗客たちが船に乗り込んでいる。
b. 羊が1匹、牧草地にいる。
c. 馬に乗った人達が羊の側にいる。
d. 前景には高い木がある。

参考 発音と位置関係の問題。
pasture 牧草地
foreground 前景
rider 乗り手

c

9.

a. その家には煙突が3本ある。
b. 窓の多くは修理が必要だ。
c. 家は売りに出されている。
d. 車道のそばに表示がある。

参考 建物の状態、背景に関する問題。
sign 標識、表示、記号、張り紙
driveway 私有車道
sold 売却済

d

10.

a. 道路は渋滞している。
b. 彼はブリッジをするのが好きだ。
c. 料金所に車はない。
d. 橋は非常に長い。

参考 風景・交通関係の発音問題。
roadway 道路
tollbooth 料金所

d

Part I 写真描写問題

11.

a. This campsite is occupied.
b. They're cooking some fish.
c. The trees are really small.
d. He's carrying a log.

12.

a. His backpack is light.
b. He's standing in the field.
c. He's looking at the valley.
d. He is trying to climb a rocky cliff.

13.

a. The sea is rough.
b. She's waving to her friend.
c. The plane is landing on the beach.
d. There are shadows on the deck.

14.

a. There's nobody in the hangar.
b. He is examining the engine.
c. The jet has just landed.
d. The man is standing on the ladder.

15.

a. They are all sitting on the grass.
b. The spectators are applauding the athlete.
c. They are listening to a concert.
d. The instruments are being cleaned.

|解答|

11.　　　　　　　　　　　　　　　　　　　　　　　a
訳 a. このキャンプ地は使用中だ。
　　b. 彼らは魚を料理している。
　　c. 木は本当に小さい。
　　d. 彼は丸太を運んでいる。

参考　全体を聞いてから判断する問題。
occupy　占領する, 塞さぐ, 陣取る
log　丸太

12.　　　　　　　　　　　　　　　　　　　　　　　c
訳 a. 彼のリュックは軽い。
　　b. 彼は野原に立っている。
　　c. 彼は谷を見ている。
　　d. 彼は岩壁をよじ登ろうとしている。

参考　人物と背景の問題。
field　野原, 分野
cliff　崖

13.　　　　　　　　　　　　　　　　　　　　　　　a
訳 a. 海は荒れている。
　　b. 彼女は友人に手を振っている。
　　c. 飛行機が海岸に着陸しているところだ。
　　d. デッキに影がある。

参考　she-seaの違いが聞き分けられるかチェックする。
wave　（動詞）手・旗を振る　（名詞）波

14.　　　　　　　　　　　　　　　　　　　　　　　b
訳 a. 格納庫には誰もいません。
　　b. 彼はエンジンを検査している。
　　c. ジェット機は着陸したところです。
　　d. 男性ははしごの上に立っています。

参考
hangar　格納庫
hanger　「えもん掛け」にも注意。
ladder　はしご

15.　　　　　　　　　　　　　　　　　　　　　　　c
訳 a. 彼らは全員が芝に座っている。
　　b. 観衆は運動選手に拍手喝采している。
　　c. 彼らはコンサートを聞いている。
　　d. 道具は掃除されている。

参考
spectator　観客
applaud　拍手喝采する
instrument　道具, 楽器

Part I 写真描写問題

16.
a. They are boarding the train.
b. The women are standing in line.
c. The cab has just stopped.
d. The wagons are in the garage.

17.
a. He's polishing the car.
b. The man is pushing the cart.
c. He's being polite.
d. The man is sweeping his yard.

18.
a. Her hand is on the microscope.
b. There are drinks on the counter.
c. The physicist is wiping the test tube.
d. The scientist is bending down.

19.
a. The sails are all up.
b. The skippers are waiting for good wind.
c. The beach is crowded with swimmers.
d. The ship is altering its course.

20.
a. The architect is drawing a blueprint.
b. One of the carpenters is about to plane a board.
c. They are talking at the construction site.
d. The building is in the foreground.

16.
a. 彼らは汽車に乗るところだ。
b. 女性達は列に並んでいる。
c. タクシーが今ちょうど止まった。
d. ワゴンは車庫にある。

> 参考 交通関係の用語。
> board 乗る
> stand in line 並ぶ
> wagon ワゴン, 貨車

解答 **a**

17.
a. 彼は車を磨いている。
b. 男性はカートを押している。
c. 彼は礼儀正しい。
d. 男性は庭を掃いている。

> 参考 発音と人物の動作の問題。
> polish 磨く
> polite 礼儀正しい
> sweep 掃く

a

18.
a. 彼女の手は顕微鏡の上に置かれています。
b. カウンターにドリンクがあります。
c. 物理学者は試験管を拭いています。
d. 科学者は上半身を曲げています。

> 参考
> microscope 顕微鏡
> physicist 物理学者
> physcian 内科医
> test tube 試験管

d

19.
a. 帆はすべて張られています。
b. 船長達は良い風を待っています。
c. 海岸は泳ぎに来ている人達で混んでいます。
d. 船は進路を変えています。

> 参考
> sail 帆
> skipper 船長
> alter 変える

a

20.
a. 建築家は設計図を描いています。
b. 大工の一人はかんなで板を削ろうとしているところです。
c. 彼らは建築現場で協議しています。
d. ビルは最前面にあります。

> 参考
> blueprint 設計図, 青写真
> plane かんな（で削る）
> construction site 建築現場
> foreground 前景, 最前面

c

Part I 写真描写問題

Part II 応答問題の攻略法

A フォーマット

Part IIは応答問題で30題あります。まず英文が1つ読まれ、それに対して3通りの応答があります。その中から最も適切な応答を1つ選びます。問題も解答も書かれていません。ビジネス関係のセンテンスを中心に，旅行やレストランの話も若干ですが出題されます。

B 問題の提示

Part IIの指示文＋例題と解答例の提示　50秒
↓
問題開始　Question number 21.（2秒）
問題文の読み上げ（約3秒）
Why did Mr. Sanchez go home early?
↓
A（3秒）(A) He left at 3:30.
↓
B（3秒）(B) He didn't feel well.
↓
C（3秒）(C) Yes, he was at home.
　　　↓（6秒）解答用のポーズ
Question number 22.（2秒）
次の問題

C 解答のコツ

解答時間は6秒です。制限時間以内に答えを選ばなければなりません。このパートでは選択肢などが書かれていませんから，特に問題文に注意を払ってください。出題の参考を知るには設問の出だしと時制を聞き取ることが大切です。そして誰がどのような応答をす

るか予測をしながら選択肢を聞いていきます。可能であればwhat, when, who, which, where, why等の疑問詞をメモします。書き付けた疑問詞を見ながら選択肢を聞き，それらの内容を確認していきます。(聞いたときにはわかってつもりでも，一瞬あとには思い出せなくなることがあります。) 選択肢A, Bを聞いて応答が正しいものだと確信できるものには○，そうでないものには×を，その可能性のあるものには△を付けCを聞いて解答を決定します。

D 傾向と対策

設問の種類としては5W1Hのほかに，否定疑問，付加疑問などにも慣れる必要があります。

特にこれら5W1H以外の形式は全体の約3分の1を占めていますから，このパートで得点を伸ばすには本書のセンテンス・パターンを口頭練習し，実際に使える会話表現として下さい。また，長いセンテンスの問題が必ず2～3問はあるので，これらを聞き，即解できるようになるために，ネイティブ向けに書かれている文章を読んだり，聞いたりする努力が必要です。(現在の目標スコアが470点までの場合は問題集で練習し，それ以上の場合は英語ニュースなどを聞いて練習してください。)

やや専門的ビジネス用語を含んだセンテンスが出題されますから本書の語句はすべて暗記してください。

Part IIがウィーク・ポイントの場合は疑問文の文頭を正確に聞き取る練習をします。(例) What did he ~?

> (1) 基本センテンス・パターンを知る
> (2) 特殊表現を覚える
> (3) ビジネス関係の語彙を強化する

■問題パターンの分析

1. 主題から連想できるが的が外れた応答をする。
   (特にwhereとwhenの問題はこれが多いように見えます。)
2. 同音異義語や類似した音の語句を使用して回答する。2～3題
3. 通常はYes/Noを予測する設問に対してYes/Noを避けた回答をする。

■ Part IIの構成

通常の疑問文	5題くらい
5W1Hの疑問文	10題くらい
（このうちwhereとwhenで始まるものが各3題くらい）	
付加疑問文	3~4題くらい
否定疑問文	2~4題くらい
（その他 why don't?の形式	2~3題くらい）
間接疑問	2題くらい
orを含んだ文章	2題くらい
その他（平常文）	出題されても1題くらい

　これらの問題文中に12単語強で構成されたやや長い文章も5題くらい出題されるのが普通だと考えられます。

■ スコア・アップのための具体策:

基本センテンス・パターンを確認する

　疑問文を聞いて瞬時に解答できるようになるには，通常の疑問文や5W1Hの疑問文のほかに，付加疑問，否定疑問にも慣れる必要があります。このために，それぞれのカテゴリーに従って問題パターンと予想できる解答を検討しておきます。

（1）付加疑問

YesとNoの区別がついているかが参考の一つとなります。

ファースト・スピーカーの本文が肯定文＋付加疑問が否定形

1. Our new president looks quite personable, doesn't he?
   新社長は好感が持てる人ですね？
   　応答が肯定的である場合
   　　Yes, he seems very friendly. 　はい，とてもフレンドリーです。
   　応答が否定の場合
   　　No, he doesn't. 　いいえ，そうは見えません。

2. The seminar last week was very interesting, wasn't it?
   先週のセミナーはとても面白かったですよね？
   　　Yes. I never thought I would enjoy it so much.
   　　はい，あれほど面白いとは思いもしませんでした。

3. Utilities have gone up recently, haven't they?
   光熱費は最近上がりましたよね？
   　Yes, by 0.5% on the average.　はい，平均して0.5％です。

4. You sent our bid for the joint venture proposal to Rome by FedEx, didn't you?
   合弁事業の申込みを国際宅急便でローマに送りましたよね？
   　Sure. Well before the due date.　もちろん。期限のずっと前に。
   　　参考　FedEx　Federal Expressの略　「国際宅急便」

5. The accountant made a mistake on this calculation, didn't she?　会計係はこの計算を間違えましたよね？
   　Right. Let me call the manager and straighten this out.
   その通りです。マネージャーを呼んでこれをちゃんとしましょう。

応答がYes/Noで始まらない場合はより一層注意して聞いてください。

6. The board meeting has been taking longer than anticipated, hasn't it?　重役会は思ったよりも時間がかかっていますよね？
   　Well, they have to come up with some kind of counter offer.
   ええと，逆提案に対して何か措置を考え出さなければならないのです。

7. The woman in the black dress is the president's sister, isn't she?　黒いドレスの女性は社長のお姉さんですよね？
   　Which one? There are so many women in black dresses.
   どの人ですか？　黒いドレスの女性は非常に多いですよ。

文末に don't you think? を付け加えて相手の同意を求めている場合もあります。

8. Sarah's got a lot of poise, don't you think?
   サラには非常に落着きがありますよね？
   　Indeed. She doesn't get upset easily.
   本当に。簡単には動揺しません。

9. Let's take a break before we finalize the deal, shall we?
　　取引をまとめる前に休憩しましょう。
　　　応答例
　　Sure. I want to stretch my legs.
　　はい。私も足を伸ばしたいです。
　　Yes, let's.　はい、そうしましょう。
　　I'm sorry I can't.　ごめんなさい。だめなのです。
　　I wish we could.　そうできればいいのですが。

本文が否定形＋付加疑問が肯定
10. What the proprietor said doesn't make sense, does it?
　　オーナーが言ったことは筋が通っていませんよね？
　　　You can say that again.　本当にそうだね。

(2) 否定疑問
YesとNoの区別がついているかがポイントの一つとなります。
通常、答えの内容が肯定的ならyes, 否定的ならnoで応答します。

肯定的応答
1. Shouldn't we postpone tomorrow's budget meeting?
　　明日の予算会議を延期するべきではありませんか。
　　　Yes. I think we should.　はい。そうするべきですね。
　　　I couldn't agree with you more.　大賛成です。

否定的応答
2. Won't you be attending the stockholders' general assembly next week?
　　来週は株主総会に出席なさらないのですか。
　　　No. I don't have time next week.
　　　いいえ。来週は時間がありません。

応答がYes/Noで始まらないケースには慣れることが必要です。
3. Isn't the merchandising seminar on May 6th?
　　販売促進のセミナーは5月6日にあるのではありませんか。
　　　According to this memo, it's on the 7th.
　　　このメモによると7日です。

4. Isn't there something strange about this letter?
   この手紙何か変ではありませんか。
      It's dated two years from now.
      日付が2年後になっています。

5. Aren't they going to approve the acquisition of the financial company?
   彼らは金融会社の買収を認めないのですか。
      I have no idea. わかりません。

6. Hasn't Ahmed finished writing his article?
   アーメッドは記事を書き終わってないのですか。
      He said he was still working on it.
      まだ取り掛かっているところだと言っていました。

7. Don't you think we should ask Sandra to revise the agenda? サンドラに議事一覧を変更してくれるように頼むべきだと思いませんか。
      What for? I think it's good enough for our meeting.
      何ですか？ 我々の会議にはこれで充分結構だと思います。

8. Won't you please have a seat? お掛けになりませんか。
      Why, thank you. おや、どうも。

9. Wasn't that the operator we talked to the other day?
   あのオペレーターは先日話した人ではありませんか。
      Maybe. そうかもしれない。

10. Wouldn't you like to go golfing with us next weekend?
    次の週末 私達といっしょにゴルフに行きませんか。
       I heard they've closed the course for renovation.
       コースは改造で閉まっているそうですよ。

(3) Why don't you..?

応答がBecauseで始まる場合
1. Why couldn't he meet the deadline for submitting the report?
   彼はどうしてレポート提出する期限に間に合わなかったのですか。
   　Because he completely forgot about it.
   その事をすっかり忘れていたからです。

ほとんどの場合，応答はBecauseで始まらない方が自然です。
2. Why don't you enroll in the next management class?
   次の経営管理のクラスに登録したらどうですか。
   　Not unless they give me an extra day off.
   もう一日余計に休みを貰えない限りはだめですね。

3. Why not trade this pickup truck in for a larger model?
   この小型トラックを下取りに出してもっと大型を買ったらどうですか。
   　I will, if I can get a good deal.
   いい条件でできるのならそうしましょう。

(4) orを使用した重文問題

A or B？の疑問文です。これは通常よりやや長い文章となります。この種の問題の聞き取りが弱点だという場合は，文章を文頭から理解するのに時間がかかり過ぎているということです。聞き取れなかった問題全文を半ば暗記するくらい繰り返しで音読し，処理スピードを上げる練習をします。

通常の応答はAまたはBのどちらかを選びます。
1. Do you want to finish the quarterly report or work on the contract draft?　四半期のレポートを終わらせたいですか，それとも契約の草案に取り掛かりますか。
   　Let me finish the report.　レポートを済まさせてください。

答えはA, Bのうちの一つとは限らない事を忘れないで下さい。

2. Are the electricians going to check the annex on Tuesday or Wednesday?
電気工が別館をチェックするのは火曜ですか水曜ですか。
　　If I'm not mistaken, it's the day after tomorrow.
もし間違っていないのなら，明後日です。

3. Who will help Mr. Booker with his work, you or Mr. Gody?
ブッカー氏の仕事を手伝うのはあなたですか，それともゴディー氏ですか。
　　Both of us.　私達二人ともです。
　　Neither. He's got his assistant.
どちらでもありません。彼にはアシスタントがいます。

4. Can you answer the phone or should I take it?
電話に出られますかそれとも私が取りましょうか。
　　It's a fax, so don't bother.
ファックスですから，かまわないで下さい。

5. What is the room rate? 250 dollars or 215 dollars?
部屋代はいくらですか。250 ドルですか，それとも 215 ドルですか。
　　Why don't you ask Mr. Sawtel? I believe he has a hotel guidebook.　ソーテルさんに聞いてみたらどうですか。ホテルのガイドブックを持っていらっしゃると思います。

6. Shall we go to the laboratory first, or drop in at our tour agent?　まず研究室に行きましょうか，それとも旅行代理店に立ち寄りましょうか。
　　We have to go to a bank before we do anything.
何をするよりも先に銀行に行かなければなりません

7. Did Mr. Lynn postpone today's meeting or will he go to the meeting directly from his place?　リン氏は今日の会議を延期するのですか，それとも自分の所から直接会議に行くのですか。
　　I don't know his schedule.
彼のスケジュールがどうなっているのかわかりません。

8. We couldn't get all the stockholders' support. Shall we cancel the purchase of the property or should we change the deal?　株主全員の支持が得られませんでした。不動産の購入を中止しましょうか，それとも取引を変更するべきですか。
   I'm afraid it's too late to do anything now.
   今何かをするには遅すぎます。

(5) What do you think …~?, Can you tell me what …?

間接疑問その他と応答例

1. Who do you think will get the top salesperson award this year?　だれが今年の最優秀セールス要員賞をもらうと思いますか。
   Either Matt or Lita.　マットかリタのどちらかでしょう。

2. Do you mind if I don't go to the seminar with you?
   あなたと一緒にセミナーに行ってもいいですか。
   Frankly speaking, I don't want to go, either.
   正直なところ，私も行きたくないのです。

3. Did you decide where you want to go for your summer vacation?　夏休みにどこに行きたいか決めましたか。
   通常の応答
   Yes. I'm going to Rome.　はい。ローマに行きます。

応答がYes/Noで始まらない例
4. Can you tell me where the town library is?
   町立図書館はどこですか。
   It's just around the corner.　角を曲がった所です。

5. How do I use this printer?
   どうやってこのプリンターを使うのですか。
   It's out of order.　故障していますよ。

(6) 発音問題

発音の聞き分けと問題の文章から連想できる応答を取り混ぜる場合

1. Why were the <u>board</u> members in such a <u>hurry</u>?
   役員達はなぜあんなに急いでいたのですか。
   They're going to <u>board</u> the plane within half an hour.
   彼らは30分以内に飛行機に搭乗するところだったのです。
   Because the man was very <u>bored</u> at the meeting.
   その男性は会議で非常に退屈していたからです。
   <u>Harry</u> introduced her to the counselors.
   ハリーは彼女をカウンセラーに紹介した。

2. How about <u>coffee</u> after the ceremony?
   式の後でコーヒーはいかがですか。
   Please make a <u>copy</u> of it before his speech.
   彼のスピーチの前にそれのコピーを作ってください。
   He was <u>coughing</u> during the meeting.
   彼は会議中に咳をしていました。

Part II

練習問題 1 — 140

まず英文が一つ読まれ、それに対して3通りの応答 a. b. c があります。
その中から最も適切な応答を 1 つ選んで○印をしてください。

1-23	1. a b c		
	2. a b c		
	3. a b c		
	4. a b c		
	5. a b c		
1-24	6. a b c		
	7. a b c		
	8. a b c		
	9. a b c		
	10. a b c		
1-25	11. a b c		
	12. a b c		
	13. a b c		
	14. a b c		
	15. a b c		
1-26	16. a b c		
	17. a b c		
	18. a b c		
	19. a b c		
	20. a b c		
1-27	21. a b c		
	22. a b c		
	23. a b c		
	24. a b c		
	25. a b c		
1-28	26. a b c		
	27. a b c		
	28. a b c		
	29. a b c		
	30. a b c		
1-29	31. a b c		
	32. a b c		
	33. a b c		
	34. a b c		
	35. a b c		
1-30	36. a b c		
	37. a b c		
	38. a b c		
	39. a b c		
	40. a b c		
1-31	41. a b c		
	42. a b c		
	43. a b c		
	44. a b c		
	45. a b c		
1-32	46. a b c		
	47. a b c		
	48. a b c		
	49. a b c		
	50. a b c		
1-33	51. a b c		
	52. a b c		
	53. a b c		
	54. a b c		
	55. a b c		
1-34	56. a b c		
	57. a b c		
	58. a b c		
	59. a b c		
	60. a b c		
1-35	61. a b c		
	62. a b c		
	63. a b c		
	64. a b c		
	65. a b c		
1-36	66. a b c		
	67. a b c		
	68. a b c		
	69. a b c		
	70. a b c		

CD					CD				
1-37	71.	a	b	c	1-44	106.	a	b	c
	72.	a	b	c		107.	a	b	c
	73.	a	b	c		108.	a	b	c
	74.	a	b	c		109.	a	b	c
	75.	a	b	c		110.	a	b	c
1-38	76.	a	b	c	1-45	111.	a	b	c
	77.	a	b	c		112.	a	b	c
	78.	a	b	c		113.	a	b	c
	79.	a	b	c		114.	a	b	c
	80.	a	b	c		115.	a	b	c
1-39	81.	a	b	c	1-46	116.	a	b	c
	82.	a	b	c		117.	a	b	c
	83.	a	b	c		118.	a	b	c
	84.	a	b	c		119.	a	b	c
	85.	a	b	c		120.	a	b	c
1-40	86.	a	b	c	1-47	121.	a	b	c
	87.	a	b	c		122.	a	b	c
	88.	a	b	c		123.	a	b	c
	89.	a	b	c		124.	a	b	c
	90.	a	b	c		125.	a	b	c
1-41	91.	a	b	c	1-48	126.	a	b	c
	92.	a	b	c		127.	a	b	c
	93.	a	b	c		128.	a	b	c
	94.	a	b	c		129.	a	b	c
	95.	a	b	c		130.	a	b	c
1-42	96.	a	b	c	1-49	131.	a	b	c
	97.	a	b	c		132.	a	b	c
	98.	a	b	c		133.	a	b	c
	99.	a	b	c		134.	a	b	c
	100.	a	b	c		135.	a	b	c
1-43	101.	a	b	c	1-50	136.	a	b	c
	102.	a	b	c		137.	a	b	c
	103.	a	b	c		138.	a	b	c
	104.	a	b	c		139.	a	b	c
	105.	a	b	c		140.	a	b	c

Part II 応答問題

Part II Scripts

1.
Who is in the room with Mr. Howard?
   a. The branch manager.
   b. He's in the back.
   c. The bookkeeper hasn't arrived.

2.
When did you join the team?
   a. Am I supposed to show my ID card?
   b. Just before I graduated.
   c. Either a driver's license or passport will do.

3.
Why don't we go out for lunch?
   a. Not until after the one p.m. meeting.
   b. We had Chinese food yesterday.
   c. Because they launched wide social reforms.

4.
Who will replace Mr. Link when he's transferred to Hawaii?
   a. As far as I know they haven't decided yet.
   b. He leaves for Hawaii in two weeks.
   c. It will be a long time before we find the ring.

5.
What time does your flight arrive in San Francisco?
   a. As soon as it lands.
   b. At 8 a.m. tomorrow.
   c. It's a quick flight to San Francisco.

スクリプト 訳

|解答|

1. 基礎知識問題　　　　　　　　　　　　　　　　　　　　　　　　a

訳　ハワード氏と部屋にいるのはだれですか。
  a. 支店長です。　　　　　　　b. 彼は後ろにいます。
  c. 帳簿係は着いていません。

参考　Who で始まる疑問文に対しての通常の答えは人名，職業名または人称代名詞。

2. 基礎知識問題　　　　　　　　　　　　　　　　　　　　　　　　b

訳　あなたはいつチームに加わったのですか。
  a. 私の身分証明書を見せる事になっているのですか。
  b. 私が卒業するちょっと前です。
  c. 運転免許証かパスポートどちらでもいいです。

参考　When に対しては時を答えるのが普通。

3. 基礎知識問題　　　　　　　　　　　　　　　　　　　　　　　　a

訳　昼食に出かけませんか？
  a. 1時のミーティングの後だったらいいです。
  b. 私たちは昨日中華料理を食べました。
  c. 彼等が広範にわたる社会改革に着手したからです。

参考　"Why don't we ~?" は「～しませんか」応答は承諾か辞退か謝絶。

4. 　　　　　　　　　　　　　　　　　　　　　　　　　　　　　　a

訳　リンク氏がハワイへ転勤するとき，誰が彼の後任になるのですか？
  a. 私が知る限りではまだ決まっていません。　b. 彼は2週間したらハワイに出発します。　c. 私達が指輪を見つけるまでにしばらくかかります。

参考　Who に対する応答の可能性は：1. 人の名前で答える。　2.「知らない」と答える。　3. 質問に答えず，逆に質問で応答する。

5. 基礎知識問題　　　　　　　　　　　　　　　　　　　　　　　　b

訳　あなたの便がサンフランシスコに到着するのは何時ですか？
  a. 着陸したらすぐです。
  b. 明日の午前8時に。
  c. サンフランシスコへの高速便です。

参考　What time に対する一般的な応答は具体的に時間を示すもの。

Part II 応答問題

6.

Hasn't Ali finished writing that article yet?
    a. He's talking on the phone now.
    b. The article is due today.
    c. He said he was still working on it.

7.

How many delegates are coming to this convention?
    a. We're expecting more than last year.
    b. Most are from Asia.
    c. Only delegates with proper identification.

8.

Those people were very helpful, weren't they?
    a. They weren't interested in it.
    b. Yes, they were.
    c. No, they aren't.

9.

Do you need to use the conference room now, or can you wait until after 3:00 p.m.?
    a. I'm afraid I'm busy now.
    b. The conference room opens after three.
    c. If it's possible, we'd like to use it before noon.

10.

Aren't you supposed to be at the seminar now?
    a. No, not until after lunch.
    b. I supported the chairman.
    c. He was opposed to it.

解答

6.   c

訳 アリはまだその記事を書き終わっていないのですか。
- a. 彼は今, 電話中です。
- b. 記事の締め切りは今日です。
- c. 彼はまだそれに取り組んでいるところだと言いました。

参考 否定疑問文の問題。応答がYes/Noで始まらない例の一つ。

7.   a

訳 この大会には何人の代表が来るのですか。
- a. 昨年より多くの参加が期待されます。 b. 大部分がアジアから来ます。
- c. 適正な身分証明書を持った代表だけです。

参考 How many に対しての典型的応答は数量を挙げますが, 具体的に数字を挙げない場合も多いので注意。 delegate「代表」

8.   b

訳 あの人たちはとても役に立ってくれましたよね。
- a. 彼らはそれに興味を持っていませんでした。
- b. はい, そうでした。
- c. いいえ, 彼らは違います。

参考 付加疑問文の問題。時制の違いが聞き取れるかどうかがポイント。

9.   c

訳 会議部屋を今使う必要があるのですか, それとも3時過ぎまで待てますか。
- a. 残念ですが今は忙しいのです。
- b. 会議部屋は, 3時過ぎに開きます。
- c. もし可能なら, 昼前にそれを使用したいのです。

参考 重文の選択問題。長い文章の速解力を試している。

10.   a

訳 現在セミナーに出席している事になっているのではありませんか。
- a. いいえ, 昼食の後までは違います。
- b. 私は会長を支持しました。
- c. 彼はそれに反対でした。

参考 否定疑問と発音の問題。not until の使い方に注意。

Part II 応答問題

11.

What did Mr. Burke's associates want to buy?
- a. The buyers were in a circle.
- b. They wanted some medical instruments.
- c. Their shipment was delivered today.

12.

Would you like me to buy you some new batteries for your recorder?
- a. No, don't re-order.
- b. I won't need it today after all.
- c. Don't bother. The thing needs to be fixed.

13.

Why did Michael quit his job so soon?
- a. As soon as possible.
- b. He felt he wasn't being treated well.
- c. He told the boss sometime yesterday.

14.

When do you expect the proposal to be approved?
- a. Not until a new vice-president is appointed.
- b. The budget will be quite high this quarter.
- c. I expect the proposal to pass.

15.

The passengers have gone through customs, haven't they?
- a. The port is slow due to renovations.
- b. It is the custom to wait for everyone.
- c. Yes, everyone is out in the arrival lobby.

11.   b

訳 バーク氏の共同経営者は何を購入したかったのですか。
- a. バイヤー達は円陣を作っていました。
- b. 彼らは医療機器がいくつか欲しかったのです。
- c. 彼らの荷は，今日，配達されました。

参考 What+基礎動詞の基本表現を理解できるかを試している。
associate「共同経営者」　medical instruments「医療機器」

12.   c

訳 あなたのレコーダー用に新しいバッテリーを買ってきましょうか。
- a. いいえ，追加注文しないで下さい。
- b. 結局, 今日は，それが必要ではありせん。
- c. 気にしないで。それは修理が必要なのです。

参考 c の The thing とはレコーダーのこと。

13.   基礎知識問題   b

訳 なぜ，マイケルはそんなにすぐに仕事をやめたのですか。
- a. できるだけすぐに。
- b. 彼は良い扱いを受けていないと感じたのです。
- c. 彼は昨日のいつか，ボスに言いました。

参考 b の応答では，なぜやめたのか理由を述べている。

14.   a

訳 提案はいつ承認されると思いますか。
- a. 新しい副社長が任命された時です。
- b. この四半期，予算は非常に高いです。
- c. 提案が承認されることを期待しています。

参考 proposal, approve, appoint など実社会で使われる単語の知識問題。

15.   c

訳 乗客達は税関を通り抜けましたよね。
- a. 修理のため港では手間がかかります。
- b. みんなを待つのが習慣です。
- c. はい，みんな到着ロビーに出ています。

参考 customs「税関」と custom「習慣」の違いを確認すること。

16.

Why are our supplies so low?

    a. It's time to order more.

    b. The truckers are on strike.

    c. Because they surprised us.

17.

Where will the union report be printed?

    a. It will be finished ahead of schedule.

    b. At the union meeting hall.

    c. On Thursday, the printers will go out on strike.

18.

What is this case made of?

    a. It's shockproof.

    b. It's guaranteed.

    c. It's plastic.

19.

Our new public relations chief looks quite personable, doesn't he?

    a. The public relations department is busy now.

    b. Yes, he's very friendly from what I hear.

    c. No, I don't know anything about his projects.

20.

How about a game of chess tonight?

    a. I'm afraid I don't have time.

    b. The game has already finished.

    c. For about three years.

| 解答

16.   b
訳 なぜ在庫がこんなに少ないのですか。
- a. もっと注文する時です。
- b. トラックの運転手たちがストライキ中なのです。
- c. 彼らは私達を驚かせました。

参考 a 質問に対して応答がうまくかみ合わない。

17.   基礎知識問題   b
訳 組合のレポートはどこで印刷されるのですか。
- a. それは予定より早く終わります。
- b. 組合の会議ホールです。
- c. 木曜日に印刷業者たちはストライキをします。

参考 where を聞き取っていれば答えられる問題。

18.   c
訳 このケースは何でできているのですか。
- a. 耐震性になっています。
- b. 保証されています。
- c. プラスチックです。

参考 素材は何かと聞かれている。shockproof「耐震性の」

19.   b
訳 新しい広報部のチーフはとても魅力的ですよね。
- a. 広報部は現在忙しいです。
- b. ええ、彼は非常にフレンドリーだと聞いています。
- c. いいえ、彼のプロジェクトについては何も知りません。

参考 personable「感じの良い、ハンサムな」

20.   基礎知識問題   a
訳 今夜、チェスはどうですか。
- a. 残念ですが時間がないのです。　b. 試合はもう終わりました。
- c. 3年間くらいです。

参考 How about + 名詞の疑問文。お誘いに対する断りの表現をさがす。game「獲物」

21.
Shall we hold the seminar here or at the new building?
    a. Let's use the new facility.
    b. I'm not in the mood for a party.
    c. A lot of the senior executives are going.

22.
Who mailed that package to the New Delhi office?
    a. I'm afraid the new secretary went to the post office.
    b. I believe Mr. Hara did.
    c. They already received it.

23.
When will our new line of products be marketed in Australia?
    a. Our market analysis will be finished soon.
    b. Our products should be very successful in Australia.
    c. In time for the Christmas season.

24.
Where are you staying in town?
    a. The convention center is close to my hotel.
    b. I made reservations for three days.
    c. At Julie's friend's place.

25.
Why don't we talk about these requests over a cup of coffee?
    a. I don't think there's time for that.
    b. These requests were written last month.
    c. The meeting room is reserved for 30 minutes.

	解答

21.   a
訳 セミナーはここでしましょうか, それとも新しいビルにしましょうか。
  a. 新しい施設を使いましょう。
  b. 私はパーティーの気分ではありません。
  c. 多くの上級管理者たちが行きます。

参考 A or B? に対する応答を優先する。

22. 基礎知識問題   b
訳 その小包をニューデリー事務所に郵送したのは誰ですか。
  a. 新しい秘書は郵便局へ行ったのではないかと思います。
  b. 原さんだと思います。
  c. 彼らはすでにそれを受け取りました。

参考 冒頭のWho mailedがわかれば解答できるはず。

23.   c
訳 当社の新製品はいつオーストラリアの市場で販売されますか。
  a. 当社の市場分析はすぐに終わります。
  b. 当社の製品はオーストラリアでに非常に成功するはずです。
  c. クリスマス・シーズンに間に合うようにです。

参考 new line「新製品」と be marketed「販売される」は必須表現。

24. 基礎知識問題   c
訳 あなたは町のどこに泊っているのですか。
  a. コンヴェンション・センターは私のホテルの近くにあります。
  b. 2泊3日の予約をしました。
  c. ジュリーの友人の所です。

参考 a は Where is the convention center? に対する応答。

25. 基礎知識問題   a
訳 コーヒーを飲みながらこれらの要請について話しませんか。
  a. その時間があるとは思いません。
  b. これらの要請は先月書かれました。
  c. 会議室の予約は30分間です。

参考 Why don't we で勧誘の文章だとわかる。b, c は応答になってない。

Part II 応答問題   69

26.

How do you think we can identify our distributor's representative when we have so many visitors in the hall?
    a. All the crew members carry identity badges.
    b. Don't worry. Our sales people can help us find the person.
    c. We can check the accounting records.

27.

Have the assembly lines been inspected?
    a. Everything is perfectly in line with company policy.
    b. All workers will assemble for a demonstration.
    c. No, but Mr. Delgado will be inspecting them tomorrow.

28.

Where can I take Spanish lessons in the evenings?
    a. Spanish is one of the most popular languages for students.
    b. You can take evening courses at the city culture center.
    c. In the evening, I like to study Spanish at home.

29.

Would you like a window or aisle seat?
    a. It doesn't matter. Either will do.
    b. I can stow my bag under my seat.
    c. They say they prefer to stand at the back.

30.

Where did you buy your snow footgear?
    a. My hobby is going hiking in the snow.
    b. At Silver Mode's at the mall.
    c. In Alaska good footgear is important because of the snow.

26. **b**

訳 ホールにこんなに多くの訪問客がいるとき、どうやって販売代理店の代表を確認できると思いますか。
  a. 乗務員全員が身分証明バッジを持っています。
  b. 心配しないで。販売部の人達がその人を探すのを手伝ってくれます。
  c. 会計記録をチェックできます。

参考 representative は crew member ではないので a は応答として不適切。

27. **c**

訳 組立てラインは点検済みですか。
  a. 全てが完全に会社の方針と一致しています。
  b. 今日、労働者たちは全員がデモをするために集合します。
  c. いいえ。でもデルガード氏が明日それらを調べます。

参考 assembly line「組立てライン」

28. **b**

訳 スペイン語の授業を夜間に受けることができるのはどこですか。
  a. スペイン語は学生には最も人気がある言語のうちの1つです。
  b. シティ・カルチャーセンターで夜間コースをとることができます。
  c. 夜間は自宅でスペイン語を学習したい。

参考 c.は Where do you want to ~?で始まる疑問文に対する応答。

29. **a**

訳 窓側の席それとも通路側の席がいいですか。
  a. それは重要ではないです、どちらでもいい。
  b. 私の席の下に私のバッグをしまえます。
  c. 彼らは後ろで立っているほうがいいと言ってます。

参考 b, c 双方ともどちらの席かを明確に答えていない。

30. **b**

訳 あなたの雪用の靴はどこで買ったのですか。
  a. 私の趣味は雪の中でハイキングすることです。
  b. モールにある Silver Mode 店です。
  c. アラスカでは雪用の良いはき物が重要です。

参考 footgear「履物」（集合名詞, 不可算名詞）

31.

Will you have time to come to the reunion?
   a. Yes, we do. By the end of the month.
   b. Yes, he comes in an hour.
   c. Yes, I'll be there for sure.

32.

When did your column in the magazine begin?
   a. I started it two years ago.
   b. For almost 13 months.
   c. This article is about yesterday's editorial.

33.

Should we take the bus or monorail?
   a. They say the bus is more convenient. It stops right in front of the entrance.
   b. I'm really not in any hurry.
   c. I took the train once. It was very crowded and uncomfortable.

34.

Don't you get tired working in Customer Relations?
   a. I get up very early every day, usually at around 5:30.
   b. Customer Relations is a very important department.
   c. As a matter of fact I do.

35.

What about putting a couch in the cafeteria?
   a. Not a good idea. There's not enough room in there.
   b. I had lunch in the cafeteria yesterday, and the day before.
   c. My brother has a very comfortable couch in his house.

		解答

31. 基礎知識問題 — c

訳 懇親会に来る時間はありますか。 a. はい，我々は月の終りまでにします。
b. はい，彼は1時間したら来ます。 c. ええ，絶対に参ります。

参考 Do you ~?, Have you ~?, Will she ~?, Should he ~? など通常の疑問文に対する応答は Yes または No で始まるものが多いですが，I don't know. I have no idea. Please ask someone else. What did you say? None of your business. I can't tell you. なども頭に入れて置く。

32. 基礎知識問題 — a

訳 雑誌のあなたのコラムは，いつ始まったのですか。
 a. 2年前にそれを始めました。
 b. ほとんど13ヵ月間です。
 c. この記事は昨日の社説に関してのものです。

参考 editorial「社説」

33. 基礎知識問題 — a

訳 バスかモノレールに乗るべきでしょうか。
 a. バスがより便利だそうです。入口の正面にちょうど停車します。
 b. 全然急いでいません。
 c. 電車に一度乗りましたが非常に混雑していて不快でした。

34. — c

訳 あなたは，顧客窓口で働くのがいやになりませんか。
 a. 私は毎日，非常に早く起きます。普通は5:30ごろです。
 b. 顧客窓口は，非常に重要な部署です。
 c. 実際，そうです。

参考 Customer Relations とは「顧客窓口（苦情処理係）」のこと。

35. 基礎知識問題 — a

訳 長イスをカフェテリアに置いてみてはいかがでしょうか。
 a. いいアイデアではありません。そこは充分なスペースがありません。
 b. 昨日と一昨日はカフェテリアで昼食を食べました。
 c. 私の兄は彼の家に非常に快適なソファーを持っています。

36.

Is that your camera?
   a. This one has a telephoto lens.
   b. I don't like cameras. I prefer video recorders.
   c. It belongs to Steve.

37.

Isn't Louis's mother a professor?
   a. His mother hired a professional gardener.
   b. No, but his father used to teach him.
   c. No, his mother is an attorney.

38.

Where can I find a supermarket open after 8 p.m.?
   a. Johnson's Market opens at eight every morning.
   b. There's one in front of Dalton Station.
   c. It will close in exactly 20 minutes.

39.

Are you looking for a house or a studio apartment?
   a. I'd like to rent a full-sized apartment.
   b. Yes, for about four months now.
   c. I'm a painter so I need a lot of sunlight.

40.

The seminar last week was very interesting, wasn't it?
   a. No, it was the second one this month.
   b. Professor Clyde spoke about foreign investments.
   c. Yes, I never thought it would be so informative.

解答

36. 　　　　　　　　　　　　　　　　　　　　　　　c

訳 それはあなたのカメラですか。
- a. これは望遠レンズがついています。
- b. 私はカメラは嫌いです。私はビデオレコーダーのほうがいいです。
- c. それは、スティーヴのです。

参考 cでは冒頭に述べられるべき No が省略されている。

37. 　　　　　　　　　　　　　　　　　　　　　　　c

訳 ルイのお母さんは教授ではありませんか。
- a. 彼の母親はプロの庭師を雇いました。
- b. いいえ、でも、彼の父が彼を教えたのでした。
- c. いいえ、彼の母は弁護士です。

参考 職業を答えている。

38. 　　　　　　　　　　　　　　　　　　　　　　　b

訳 午後8時以後も開いているスーパーマーケットはどこですか。
- a. ジョンソンのマーケットは、毎朝8時に開きます。
- b. ドルトン駅の前に1つあります。
- c. それは、ちょうど20分したら閉まります。

参考 a も c も when または what time で始まる質問に対する応答。

39. 　　　　　　　　　　　　　　　　　　　　　　　a

訳 家を探しているのですか、それともワンルーム・マンションですか。
- a. 私はまともな大きさのアパートを貸りたいのです。
- b. はい、現在までにおよそ4ヵ月の間です。
- c. 私は画家ですから日光がたくさん必要です。

参考 studio apartment「ワンルーム・マンション」

40. 　　　　　　　　　　　　　　　　　　　　　　　c

訳 先週のセミナーは非常に面白かったですね。
- a. いいえ、それは今月、第二回目のものでした。
- b. クライド教授は海外投資について話しました。
- c. はい。あれほど有益だとは思いませんでした。

参考 c. Yes で肯定し、続いてセミナーについての印象を述べている。

41.

Who is planning Ramon's retirement party?
  a. Ramon will retire at age 65.
  b. The people in the accounting department are.
  c. The last party was held in an Indian restaurant.

42.

What did you think of the trade fair?
  a. It took me over three hours to get there.
  b. It was more interesting than I expected.
  c. I've always believed fair trade is a good idea.

43.

Have the other tour members showed up yet?
  a. The deadline is six o'clock.
  b. Some couples are already here; they're sitting in the lobby.
  c. Drinks and snacks are now being served in the lounge.

44.

She was the same operator we talked to the other day, wasn't she?
  a. The operator gently guided the forklift to the loading dock.
  b. The other day I was in our Rome office.
  c. Maybe. Her voice sounded very familiar.

45.

Do you have to take flight 332?
  a. It leaves at 7 a.m., so she has to get up early.
  b. Yes, I have to make it to the symposium by 1:00 p.m.
  c. No, it needs to be cleaned and refueled.

| 解答 |

41. 基礎知識問題   b
訳 ラモンの引退パーティーはだれが計画しているのですか。
 a. ラモンは65歳で引退します。
 b. 会計部の人々です。
 c. この前のパーティーはインド料理店で開かれました。

参考 who で始まる質問だが，応答の主語がラモンとは考えられない。

42. 基礎知識問題   b
訳 あなたは見本市をどう思いましたか。
 a. そこに着くのに3時間かかりました。 b. それは私が期待していたより面白かったです。 c. 私はいつも公正取引は良い考えだと思っています。

参考 相手の受けた印象を聞く質問には 1. 良かった。2. 良くなかった。3. うまくコメントを避ける。の3パターンを考慮する。

43.   b
訳 ほかのツアーメンバーたちは来ていますか。
 a. 最終期限は6時です。
 b. 何カップルかはもうここにいます，彼らはロビーに座っています。
 c. ドリンクと軽食は今ラウンジで出されています。

参考 deadline とは記事などの締切日や最終受付日，期日

44.   c
訳 あの人は先日私たちが話したオペレーターと同一人物ですよね。
 a. オペレーターは徐々にフォークリフトを積み込み専用ドックに誘導した。
 b. 先日，私は当社のローマ事務所にいました。
 c. そうかも。彼女の声にはとても聞き覚えがあるような気がしました。

参考 familiar「見慣れた，聞きなれた」 familiarize「習熟する」も覚える。

45.   b
訳 あなたは332便に乗らなければなりませんか。
 a. それは午前7時に出ますから，彼女は早起きしなければなりません。
 b. はい，私はシンポジウムに間に合わせて午後1時00分までに着かなければなりません。 c. いいえ。それは清掃と燃料の補給が必要です。

参考 a は主語が「彼女」になっているので不適切。

Part II 応答問題   77

46.

Who should explain the changes to the Chairman after the contract has been revised?
- a. The Chairman is a contract lawyer himself.
- b. Ms. Neylon revised the contract.
- c. The assistant manager will.

47.

When will dinner be served?
- a. In a few minutes, right after the toast.
- b. We're having roast chicken and potatoes.
- c. I heard there was a fire in the kitchen tonight.

48.

Does he have to listen to the radio now?
- a. She's been typing since she got home this afternoon.
- b. We ought to ask him to turn the volume down.
- c. A lot of practice is necessary to be proficient.

49.

The strategy meeting is taking longer than anticipated, isn't it?
- a. Yes, one of the trustees said they finished it within 30 minutes.
- b. They're trying to come up with a response to the counter offer.
- c. I wonder whose idea it was in the first place.

50.

Can you stay late at the front desk next week?
- a. Yes, if there are no problems with my children.
- b. No, I couldn't say such a thing.
- c. I need a definite answer by next week.

		解答

46. 基礎知識問題 　　　　　　　　　　　　　　　　　　　　c

訳　契約が修正されたあと，誰が変更を会長に説明するべきですか。
  a. 会長は契約弁護士です。
  b. ニーロンさんが契約を修正しました。
  c. 課長補佐がそうします。

参考　主語と動詞まではっきり聞き取れているかを試している。

47. 基礎知識問題 　　　　　　　　　　　　　　　　　　　　a

訳　夕食の用意はいつできますか。
  a. 2〜3分したらです。乾杯の直後。　b. ロースト・チキンとジャガイモを食べよう。　c. 今夜，台所で火事があったと聞きました。

参考　When willで始まる質問に対する答えは1.今から，2.すでに始まっている，または終わっている，3.未来時制で答える，4.わからない，の4パターンが考えられる。

48. 　　　　　　　　　　　　　　　　　　　　　　　　　　b

訳　彼は今，ラジオを聞かなければならないのですか。
  a. 今日の午後家に帰った時から，彼女はタイプしています。
  b. 私達は彼にボリュームを下げるよう頼むべきです。
  c. 熟達するには練習がたくさん必要です。

参考　質問の真意：「ラジオがうるさいので音を下げるように」

49. 　　　　　　　　　　　　　　　　　　　　　　　　　　b

訳　戦略会議は思ったより時間がかかっていますね。
  a. はい。理事の一人は，彼らはそれを30分以内に終えたと言いました。
  b. 彼らは修正申込みへの対応を考え出そうとしています。
  c. まず，それが誰の考えだったのかと思います。

参考　trustee「大学の理事，管財人」

50. 　　　　　　　　　　　　　　　　　　　　　　　　　　a

訳　来週，フロント係の残業ができますか。
  a. はい。子供達が大丈夫ならできます。
  b. いいえ。そのようなことは言えませんでした。
  c. 私は来週までに明確な答えが必要です。

参考　a 子供達に何か問題があればできないが，そうでない限りはできる。

Part II 応答問題

51.

Isn't the cast supposed to change each month?
- a. Yes, the doctor will change the cast.
- b. Yes, but only if there is an emergency.
- c. No, every three months.

52.

Our utilities have gone up recently, haven't they?
- a. Only when the employees work overtime.
- b. We try to utilize everything to the maximum.
- c. Yes, by 1.5% on the average.

53.

The woman in the black dress is the president's wife, isn't she?
- a. Which one? There are so many women in black dresses.
- b. The president's wife attends all company social functions.
- c. Black dresses are considered very fashionable these days.

54.

How would you like to take a look at the new trucks before we send them to our branch offices?
- a. I understand we got them at a discount.
- b. New trucks should speed up our operations by 15%.
- c. I've been wanting to do that. Where are they?

55.

Could I leave a message for your father?
- a. My father's eyesight is really bad recently.
- b. OK, but he won't be back until next week.
- c. Why don't you call back when he's out of town?

解答

51.   c
訳 キャストは，毎月変わることになっていませんか。
 a. はい，お医者さんはギプスを替えます。
 b. はい，非常事態の場合のみです。
 c. いいえ，3ヵ月ごとです。

参考 cast「配役，ギプス，（動詞）投げる」

52.   c
訳 我々の光熱費が最近上がりましたよね。
 a. 従業員が時間外に働くときだけ。
 b. 我々は，すべてを最大限に利用しようとする。
 c. はい。平均して1.5%です。

参考 utilities「光熱費，用益費，公共施設，公益事業」

53.   a
訳 黒いドレスを着た女性は社長の奥様ですよね。
 a. どの人ですか。黒いドレスを着た女性はすごくたくさんいますよ。
 b. 社長の奥様は会社の全社交的行事に出席します。
 c. 黒いドレスは，最近，非常ファッショナブルだと思われています。

参考 直接的解答をしないで人物特定のために疑問文で対応する例。
fashionable「しゃれている，流行の，上流社会の」

54.   c
訳 新しいトラックを支社に送る前にそれらを見たいでしょうか。
 a. 割引価格でそれらを得たと理解しています。
 b. 新しいトラックは我々の操業速度を15%上げるはずです。
 c. ずっとそうしたいと思っていました，どこにあるのですか。

参考 How would you like ～しませんか

55.   基礎知識問題   b
訳 あなたのお父様に伝言を残せますか。
 a. 最近，父の視力が非常に良くないのです。
 b. OK，でも彼は来週まで帰りませんよ。
 c. 彼が町の外にいる時に電話をかけ直したらどうですか。

参考 電話応答問題での基礎的会話をチェックしてみよう。

56.

How can I improve my translation skills?

    a. By studying other translators' work.

    b. Well, I improved my computer skills by taking night classes.

    c. Translation is an ability that requires great effort.

57.

Why don't you use staples instead of tape for putting up the posters?

    a. These posters explain all about safety on the factory floor.

    b. Paul borrowed my stapler and hasn't returned it yet.

    c. When I use tape the posters usually fall down.

58.

Are the executives' photos in the middle or on the last page of the annual report?

    a. They should be on the second page.

    b. This year we had the executive photos done in color.

    c. The middle of the annual report has the company history.

59.

Can you tell me how to use the new printer?

    a. Why don't you ask Peter? He knows all about it.

    b. The printer is used, so we don't have a manual.

    c. I don't know anything about data processing.

60.

What's the purpose of your visit?

    a. I propose to leave as soon as possible.

    b. I'm here to see my relatives.

    c. I'll stay for about 15 days.

解答

56.   a

訳 私はどうしたら翻訳の腕を磨くことがことができますか。
　　a. 他の翻訳者達の作品を研究する事でできます。
　　b. ええと, 私は夜間クラスでコンピュータ技術を磨きました。
　　c. 翻訳は非常な努力を要する能力です。

参考 how に対しては方法を答える。

57.   b

訳 ポスターを掲示するのにテープではなくてホチキスを使ったらどうですか。
　　a. これらのポスターは工場フロアでの安全についての全てを説明しています。
　　b. ポールが私のホチキスを借りて, まだ返していません。
　　c. テープを使うと普通はポスターが落ちます。

参考 b ホチキスが手元にないので他の方法で掲示している。

58.   a

訳 重役の写真は年次報告の真中に入れますか, または巻末ページにしますか。
　　a. それらは第2ページに載せるべきです。
　　b. 今年は重役の写真をカラーにしました。
　　c. 年次報告の中央には会社史が載っています。

参考 A or B? の問に対して, もう1つ別の選択肢を指示したもの。

59.   a

訳 新しいプリンターの使い方を教えてくれますか。
　　a. ピーターに頼んでみたらどうです。それに関しては彼がとてもよく知っています。　　b. プリンターは中古なので, 我々にはマニュアルがありません。　　c. 私は情報処理について何も知りません。

参考 b マニュアルがあるかを質問しているわけではないので不適切。

60.   基礎知識問題   b

訳 あなたの訪問の目的はなんですか。
　　a. 私はできるだけ早く出ることを提案します。
　　b. 私はここに, 親戚に会いに来ました。
　　c. 15日間くらいいます。

参考 b の他に sightseeing, business, study, conference 等も考えられる。

61.

You're from Germany, aren't you?

    a. I've been there several times.

    b. Actually, I'm an Italian living in Germany.

    c. Yes, she has a German accent.

62.

Where can I find a nice restaurant?

    a. I found one yesterday.

    b. In about five minutes.

    c. There's one right around the corner.

63.

Do you think we should get in touch with our lawyer, or what?

    a. We didn't touch anything until the lawyers arrived.

    b. Have the secretary call him at once.

    c. What is it you want to do?

64.

Why was the committee meeting rescheduled?

    a. Rescheduling is entirely up to the members of the committee.

    b. The schedule has not been changed for years.

    c. Some of the members had to meet the delegation from Korea at the airport.

65.

Have you used the latest statistical software yet?

    a. Yes, it was great. It gives you results instantaneously.

    b. I could never understand statistics.

    c. It cost a lot of money. I hope it's worth it!

61.　　　　　　　　　　　　　　　　　　　　b

[訳] あなたはドイツの出身ですよね。
- a. 私は何度かそこに行った事があります。
- b. 実際は，私はドイツに住んでいるイタリア人です。
- c. ええ。彼女にはドイツ語訛りがあります。

[参考] b. Actually「実際は」という語でドイツ出身を否定している。

62.　基礎知識問題　　　　　　　　　　　　　c

[訳] どこかに良いレストランがありますか。
- a. 昨日1つ見つけました。
- b. 5分くらいしてから。
- c. 角を曲がった所に1軒あります。

[参考] right around the corner は頻出表現

63.　　　　　　　　　　　　　　　　　　　　b

[訳] 当社の弁護士と連絡を取るべきだと思いますか，それとも何か他のことがありますか。
- a. 弁護士が到着するまでは何にも触れなかった。
- b. 秘書に，すぐ彼に電話をかけさせてください。
- c. あなたは何をしたいのですか。

[参考] get in touch「連絡する」　keep in touch「連絡を絶やさないでおく」

64.　　　　　　　　　　　　　　　　　　　　c

[訳] 委員会の日程はどうして変更されたのですか。
- a. 予定の組み直しは，すべて委員会のメンバーによります。
- b. 予定は何年も変わっていません。
- c. メンバーの何人かが，空港で韓国の代表団を出迎えなければなりませんでした。

[参考] 選択肢aは，時制が現在であり，質問の解答としては相応しくない。

65.　基礎知識問題　　　　　　　　　　　　　a

[訳] あなたは，もう最新の統計のソフトウェアを使いましたか。
- a. それは素晴らしかったです。それは即座に結果を出します。
- b. 統計が全然理解できませんでした。
- c. それは大変な金額でした。それなりの価値があることを望みます！

[参考] statistics「統計，統計学」a が一番素直な応答。

66.

When is June getting married?
   a. Not until she loses 20 pounds.
   b. To a man who is a dentist.
   c. At a small church in her hometown.

67.

Where can I call to order some pizza?
   a. There's a fast delivery company on 43rd Street.
   b. Chinese food is quite popular for take out.
   c. There's a list of places that deliver on the refrigerator.

68.

What do you estimate the TV spots will cost?
   a. Approximately $50,000 per show.
   b. Last year's estimations were much higher.
   c. Most likely, the TV spots will be cost effective.

69.

Should I go ahead and get a present for the boss, or do you want to?
   a. Let's present him with something unique this time.
   b. I'd appreciate it if you could do it.
   c. I know his birthday is next month. May 7th, I believe.

70.

How did your audition go?
   a. I guess I'm out of luck; no one has called yet.
   b. It went until almost 6:30.
   c. I'm not very good at addition.

|解答|

66.   a
訳 ジューンはいつ結婚するのですか。
- a. 彼女が20ポンド体重を減らしてからです。
- b. 歯科医である男性と。
- c. 彼女の故郷の小さい教会で。

参考 Whenを聞き取るのがポイント。Not untilの表現に注意すること。

67.   c
訳 ピザを注文するにはどこに電話をすればいいですか。
- a. 43番街に急配会社があります。
- b. 中華料理は，お持ち帰り用の食品として人気があります。
- c. 冷蔵庫の上に出前してくれる所のリストがあります。

参考 a delivery companyは出前をするレストランではない。

68.   a
訳 テレビのスポット広告はいくらかかると見積もりますか。
- a. 一回につき約50,000ドルです。
- b. 去年の見積りは，もっと高かったです。
- c. 多分，テレビのスポット広告は費用効率が高いです。

参考 estimate「見積もる」　TV spot = spot advertisementのこと。

69. 基礎知識問題   b
訳 私が行ってボスへのプレゼントを買って来るべきですか，それともあなたがそうしたいですか。
- a. 今回は彼に何かユニークなものを贈りましょう。
- b. あなたがそうして下されば，有難いです。
- c. 彼の誕生日は来月，5月7日だと思います。

参考 I'd appreciate it if you could ～ は慣用的表現。要暗記。

70.   a
訳 あなたのオーディションの出来はどうでした？
- a. 私には運がなかったと思います。まだ誰も電話をかけてきませんから。
- b. それは，ほとんど6時半まで続きました。
- c. 私は足し算が得意ではありません。

参考 物事がうまくいかなかったことを婉曲的に述べている。

Part II 応答問題

71.

The janitor has replaced the light bulbs, hasn't he?
- a. Vandals broke over 20 bulbs.
- b. The janitor has been all over the building.
- c. He's been too busy to do it.

72.

Who do I speak to about making arrangements for our guests to tour the plant?
- a. The foreman has to water the plant first.
- b. Since Mr. Guerrero is away, I'm the person.
- c. All guests must wear hard hats and goggles while on tour.

73.

Wasn't Ms. Webber in Berlin three days ago?
- a. Three days ago Berlin was fogged in.
- b. Yes, she was escorting some of our retailers to the factory there.
- c. No, Ms. Webber works for a German bank.

74.

When is your coffee break?
- a. It's usually at ten, but I want to finish this report first.
- b. I'll go whether you come or not.
- c. The coffee machine is turned on all day.

75.

When can we meet to discuss our new bid?
- a. The day before yesterday was convenient for me.
- b. I propose we do it until I return.
- c. I don't have anything scheduled tomorrow morning after 10:30.

71.　　　　　　　　　　　　　　　　　　　　　c

訳 管理人は電球を取り替えましたよね。
- a. 公共物を壊す人達が球を20個以上も壊しました。
- b. 管理人が建物のいたる所に行きました。
- c. 彼は忙し過ぎてそれをする事が出来なかったのです。

参考 janitor「管理人」　vandal「芸術，公共物，自然，文化の破壊者」

72.　　　　　　　　　　　　　　　　　　　　　b

訳 お客様のために工場ツアーの手配をするには誰に話せばいいですか。
- a. 主任は最初に植物に水をやらなければなりません。
- b. ゲレロ氏が外出中ですから，私です。
- c. ツアーの間，お客様はヘルメットとゴーグルを着用します。

参考 hard hat「ヘルメット」　goggles「ゴーグル」

73.　　　　　　　　　　　　　　　　　　　　　b

訳 ウェバーさんは3日前ベルリンにいませんでした？
- a. 三日前，ベルリンは霧で覆われていました。
- b. はい。彼女は当社の小売業者数人に付き添って，そこの工場に行きました。
- c. いいえ。ウェバーさんはドイツの銀行で働いています。

参考 retailer「小売業者」　wholesaler「卸業者」　escort「付き添う」

74.　　　　　　　　　　　　　　　　　　　　　a

訳 あなたのコーヒーブレークはいつですか。
- a. 通常は10時ですが，まずこのレポートを終えたいのです。
- b. あなたが来るかどうかに関係なく，私は行きます。
- c. コーヒー・マシンは一日中ついています。

参考 a 休憩時間にコーヒーブレークを取らない理由を述べている。

75.　　　　　　　　　　　　　　　　　　　　　c

訳 当社の新しい入札について協議するのに，いつお会いできますか。
- a. 私にとっては一昨日が好都合でした。
- b. 私が戻るまでに私たちがそれをすることを提案します。
- c. 明朝の10時半以降はなにも予定がありません。

参考 I don't have anything scheduled ～ は覚える事。

76.

The clerk could have made a mistake on Mr. Miller's hotel charges, couldn't she?

    a. Right. Let me call the manager and straighten it out.

    b. Mr. Miller always keeps all of his expense receipts.

    c. That hotel is one of the best in the city; we've been using it for years.

77.

Who will be helping Mr. Misawa with his demonstration of the accounting software?

    a. Mr. Misawa has given many software demonstrations before.

    b. Ms. Matsushita said she would assist him, since she's available on that day.

    c. With this we should be able to cut costs considerably.

78.

What the proprietor said doesn't make any sense, does it?

    a. Yes, they made the scene.

    b. He gave a speech appropriate for the occasion.

    c. You can say that again.

79.

How about getting together after the seminar for a bite?

    a. I'd be delighted. I could use some fresh air too.

    b. He raised some interesting cases of joint ventures.

    c. Before the seminar the custodian turned on a light.

80.

What do you think the president will buy his wife for their silver anniversary?

    a. It's their 25th wedding anniversary gift.

    b. We'll just have to wait and see!

    c. He'll probably buy it at a major department store.

76.   a

訳 従業員は，ミラー氏のホテル代金を間違えたかもしれませんね。
　a. その通りです。マネージャーに電話してそれを正しましょう。
　b. ミラー氏は，常に出費の領収書を全部とっておきます。　c. そのホテルはこの都市で最高のうちの1つです，我々は長年それを使っています。

参考 典型的なヒッカケ問題。疑問文中に使われている語句や名前が全く言い換えられることなく使われているものは正答の確率が低い。

77.   b

訳 会計ソフトの実演では誰が三沢氏を手伝うのですか。
　a. 三沢はソフトウェア実演を何度も行った事があります。
　b. 松下さんは，その日手が空いているので彼を手伝うと言いました。
　c. これで，弊社は，かなりのコスト削減ができるはずです。

参考 demonstration「実演，実物宣伝」

78.   c

訳 所有者が言ったことは全く筋が通っていませんよね。
　a. はい。彼らは現れました。
　b. 彼はその場にふさわしいスピーチをしました。
　c. 全く君が言う通りだ。

参考 cの表現は暗記すること。make a scene「醜態を演じる」に注意。

79. 基礎知識問題   a

訳 セミナーの後，いっしょに軽い食事でもどうですか。
　a. 喜んで。私もちょっと新鮮な空気を吸いたいですからね。
　b. 彼は合併事業の面白い例をいくつか持ち出した。
　c. セミナーの前に管理人がライトをつけた。

参考 aは必須表現　I need to stretch my legs. も同様の場合に使う表現。

80.   b

訳 社長は自分たちの銀婚式用に奥さんに何を買うと思いますか。
　a. 彼らの第25回目の結婚記念の贈り物です。
　b. 時がくればわかりますよ。
　c. 彼は多分，主要デパートでそれを買いますよ。

参考 b「まだわからない」の意。

81.

Where do you want me to put the estimate?
   a. Don't leave until Thursday afternoon.
   b. On Mr. Hurley's desk. He is the chief accountant.
   c. We think he paid $3,500 for the new motorbike.

82.

How much will it cost to have a jacket custom made?
   a. I suppose at least 400 dollars.
   b. It depends on the price.
   c. They make custom clothes really cheap in Bangkok.

83.

Why haven't we been getting any mail at the office?
   a. We already have six males at this office, and two females.
   b. I saw the mailman across the street.
   c. I don't know. I'll check with the post office.

84.

Isn't the shipment due a week from today?
   a. The shipyard is closed for the day.
   b. We fill out the shipping form and send it to the transportation manager.
   c. They changed it to the end of the month.

85.

Isn't the first round of negotiations with management supposed to end before May?
   a. I hope so, but it doesn't look like it.
   b. May is one of the best times to drive around.
   c. Management was supposed to let us know.

解答

81.　　　　　　　　　　　　　　　　　　　　　　　　　　b

訳 どこに見積もりを置いてもらいたいのですか。
  a. 木曜日の午後まで出発しないで下さい。
  b. ハーリー氏の机の上に。彼が会計主任です。
  c. 彼は新しいオートバイを買うのに3,500ドルを支払ったと思います。

参考 estimate「見積書」

82.　基礎知識問題　　　　　　　　　　　　　　　　　　　a

訳 ジャケットをあつらえるのにいくらかかりますか。
  a. 少なくとも400ドルかかると思います。
  b. それは価格によります。
  c. バンコクでは本当に安く注文服を作ります。

参考 have ~ custom made「あつらえる」

83.　　　　　　　　　　　　　　　　　　　　　　　　　　c

訳 どうして私達はオフィスで全然メールを受け取れていないのですか。
  a. このオフィスではすでに男性6人と女性2人がいます。
  b. 通りの向こう側に郵便集配人を見ました。
  c. わかりません、郵便局で調べてみます。

参考 Whyに対応する可能性は；1. 理由を述べる　2.「わからない」

84.　　　　　　　　　　　　　　　　　　　　　　　　　　c

訳 出荷の期限は、来週の今日ではありませんか。
  a. 造船所は本日の営業を終えました。
  b. 出荷用紙に記入して、輸送部マネージャーに送ります。
  c. 月末に変更になりました。

参考 closed for the day は必須表現

85.　　　　　　　　　　　　　　　　　　　　　　　　　　a

訳 経営陣との第1回目交渉は5月前に終わることになっていませんか。
  a. そう願っていますが、そのようには見えません。
  b. 5月は、ドライブするのに一番良い時期の1つです。
  c. 経営陣は我々に知らせるはずでした。

参考 全てを聴いて、時制を決め手に判断する。

86.
Have you compared the prices of cellular phones recently?
- a. They can be a major expense for some businesses.
- b. They're more reasonable at discount stores.
- c. It's not that expensive.

87.
What if our subsidiary outgrows us?
- a. Under the circumstances we have to put off the campaign.
- b. That'll be the day.
- c. Let's call it a day.

88.
Would it be OK if we gave them some background information on our production methods?
- a. The infrastructure will be rebuilt within five years.
- b. Why not? It can't hurt.
- c. Our production methods are standard for the industry.

89.
Do you have any idea which organization is going to be the sponsor of the event next year?
- a. The sponsor will decide where the convention will be held.
- b. Yes, the convention will be in Sapporo next year.
- c. They say one of the local TV stations.

90.
What's the fastest way to get to City General Hospital from here?
- a. I can drive you there.
- b. Yes. An ambulance is on the way.
- c. The hospital is next to Highway 94.

	解答

86.   **b**
訳 最近携帯電話の価格を比較しましたか。
   a. それは数社にとっては大きな出費となります。
   b. 安売り店ではより手ごろな値段です。
   c. それはそんなに高いわけではありません。

参考 比較した結果を答えている。

87.   **b**
訳 我々の子会社が我々より大きくなったらどうだろう？
   a. このような状況のもとでは，キャンペーンを延期しなければならない。
   b. そんな事ありえない。
   c. 今日はこれで切り上げよう。

参考 b. c. は表現自体の知識を問われている。両方とも覚えよう。

88.   **b**
訳 弊社の生産方法に関する背景情報を彼らに与えてもよろしいでしょうか。
   a. 基礎構造は5年以内に再建されます。
   b. もちろん。それが害になることはないですよ。
   c. 弊社の生産方法がこの産業の標準になっています。

参考 Would it be OK if ~ 「～してもよろしいでしょうか」

89.   **c**
訳 どの組織が来年のイベントのスポンサーになるかわかりますか。
   a. スポンサーが大会の開催場所を決めます。
   b. はい。大会は札幌であります。   c. その土地のテレビ局の1つだそうです。

参考 Do you have any idea which organization までをしっかり聞き取れない場合はこの疑問文を5秒以内で言えるまで口頭練習すること。

90.   **a**
訳 ここから市立総合病院に行くのに最も速い方法はなんですか。
   a. 私はあなたをそこに乗せて行くことができます。
   b. はい。救急車が1台，向かっています。
   c. その病院は，ハイウェー94の隣にあります。

参考 general hospital「総合病院」   ambulance「救急車」

91.
Who is in charge of petty cash, John Lee or Janet Simmons?
    a. They cashed the check at the department store.
    b. I think John has already gone home.
    c. Neither. Mrs. Madison is.

92.
Why don't we continue this discussion of the new design over breakfast tomorrow?
    a. I don't know what will be on the breakfast menu tomorrow.
    b. The designer doesn't get back till the end of this month.
    c. That's fine with me. We can sleep on it, then.

93.
Where is the key to the cabinet?
    a. Mrs. Goodwin always keeps it in her purse.
    b. The cabinet was always unlocked.
    c. Ricky was the last one to open the cabinet.

94.
Mr. Yuma has been appointed head of Human Resources, hasn't he?
    a. The head of Human Resources has recently retired.
    b. You mean you didn't know? A memo was put out three days ago.
    c. Any new appointments must be approved by the Board.

95.
Did my client leave his number when he was here?
    a. Your client waited for almost an hour.
    b. Not that I know of.
    c. Do you know your client's phone number?

解答

91. 基礎知識問題　　c

訳 小口現金の責任者は誰ですか，ジョン・リーそれともジャネット・シモンズですか。

　a. 彼等はその小切手をデパートで現金化しました。　b. ジョンはすでに家に帰りました。　c. どちらでもありません。マディソン夫人です。

参考 petty cash「小口現金」　petty cashier「小口現金係り」

92.　　c

訳 明日，朝食を取りながら新デザインに関しての話し合いを続けませんか。

　a. 何が明日朝食メニューに入っているか知りません。
　b. デザイナーは今月末まで戻って来ません。
　c. それでいいです。それでは一晩考えましょう。

参考 sleep on it は必須表現

93. 基礎知識問題　　a

訳 キャビネットのカギはどこにありますか。

　a. グッドウィン夫人が常に彼女の財布に入れています。
　b. キャビネットにはいつもカギがかかっていませんでした。
　c. リッキーがキャビネットを開けた最後の人でした。

参考 purse「財布」　文頭の where が聞き取れていれば解答できるはず。

94.　　b

訳 ユマ氏は人事部の長に指名されましたよね。

　a. 人事部長は最近引退しました。
　b. あなたは知らなかったのですか。メモは3日前に出ていたのですよ。
　c. 新しい任命はすべて，重役会で承認されなければなりません。

参考 be appointed「指名される」　be nominated「指名される」

95. 基礎知識問題　　b

訳 私のクライアントはここにいたとき電話番号を置いていきましたか。

　a. あなたのクライアントは，ほとんど1時間近く待ちました。
　b. 私が知る限りではそういうことはありません。
　c. あなたのクライアントの電話番号を知っていますか。

参考 b. の Not that I know of. は必須表現。

96.

Who will be replacing our liaison while she's on vacation next week?

    a. I'll be going next week, too.

    b. All of the advertising staff will take over her duties.

    c. The job of liaison is very difficult; not just anyone can do it.

97.

Won't you be attending the stockholders' general meeting next week?

    a. No, I don't have time next week.

    b. Attendance will probably be very high.

    c. The stockholders are meeting at exactly ten o'clock.

98.

Have you checked the latest weather forecast?

    a. I'm sorry, I got drenched.

    b. No, it rained all week.

    c. Yes, it's going to be cloudy.

99.

It's all right to leave my newspaper on the tour bus, isn't it?

    a. Yes, but please bring your valuables with you.

    b. We'll only be stopping for about ten minutes.

    c. No, but I like reading magazines.

100.

When will Mr. Norton return from his business trip?

    a. He'll be back before Thanksgiving Day.

    b. Mr. Norton has a round trip ticket.

    c. Anytime should be fine.

96.　　　　　　　　　　　　　　　　　　　　　　　　　b

訳 来週彼女が休暇の間は誰が代って交渉係になるのですか。
　a. 私も来週行きます。　　b. 広告部門のスタッフが全員で彼女の仕事を引き受けます。　　c. 交渉係の仕事は非常に難しいです，誰でもそれをできるというわけではありません。

参考 replace「代りになる」　liaison section「渉外課」

97.　　　　　　　　　　　　　　　　　　　　　　　　　a

訳 来週，株主総会に出席なさらないのですか。
　a. いいえ。来週は時間がありません。
　b. 出席は多分非常に多いでしょう。
　c. 株主達は，ちょうど10時に会っています。

参考 attendance「出席数」　turnout「出席数」も要注意。

98.　基礎知識問題　　　　　　　　　　　　　　　　　　　c

訳 最新の天気予報をチェックしましたか。
　a. すみません，私はずぶ濡れになりました。
　b. いいえ。一週間ずっと雨が降りました。
　c. はい。曇りになります。

参考 b. は今後の天気予報ではなく過去の事実を述べているので不適切。

99.　　　　　　　　　　　　　　　　　　　　　　　　　a

訳 ツアーバスに私の新聞を置いておいていいですよね。
　a. はい。でも貴重品はお持ちください。
　b. およそ10分止まるだけです。
　c. いいえ。でも私は雑誌を読むのが好きです。

参考 バスの中でガイドが言うこと。

100.　　　　　　　　　　　　　　　　　　　　　　　　a

訳 ノートン氏はいつ出張から戻りますか。
　a. 感謝祭前に戻ります。
　b. ノートン氏は往復旅行チケットを持っています。
　c. いつでもいいと思います。

参考 When と時制で判断する。

Part II 応答問題

101.

Who met with the new CEO after the luncheon?

    a. Your guess is as good as mine.

    b. The new CEO enjoys meeting people.

    c. Most of the staff members came to the luncheon.

102.

The team has been in Japan before, hasn't it?

    a. This isn't the last time.

    b. Teams from other countries often play in Japan.

    c. They played here in 1998.

103.

Who is your partner's new assistant?

    a. I think this department is overstaffed.

    b. She's my cousin, Ellie Perlman.

    c. My partner's assistant was Ron McCarthy.

104.

Perhaps some of my customers would like to come to the reception.

    a. Don't count them out.

    b. Actually, we were hoping they would.

    c. The reception hall can seat 200 people.

105.

Why haven't the names of the new managers been announced yet?

    a. Over 20 managers have been promoted.

    b. I couldn't agree with you more.

    c. Everything is subject to the decision of the Board at the next meeting.

| 解答 |

101.   **a**

訳 昼食後に新しいCEOと会ったのは誰ですか。
- a. 私も知らないのです。
- b. 新しいCEOは人々に会うのを楽しんでいます。
- c. スタッフ・メンバーの多くが昼食に来ました。

参考 Your guess is as good as mine. は覚えておきたい表現。

102.   **c**

訳 チームは以前に日本にきましたね。
- a. 今回が最後ではありません。
- b. 外国からやって来たチームがたびたび日本でプレーします。
- c. 1998年にここでプレーしました。

参考 Yes/No で答えずに事実を述べて肯定している。

103. 基礎知識問題   **b**

訳 あなたのパートナーの新しいアシスタントは，誰ですか。
- a. この部署は人員過剰だと思います。
- b. 彼女は私のいとこのエリー・パールマンです。
- c. 私のパートナーのアシスタントは，ロン・マッカーシーでした。

参考 overstaffed「人員過剰の」　understaffed「人員不足の」

104.   **b**

訳 多分，私の顧客なかにはレセプションに来たい人がいると思います。
- a. 彼らを参加人数から外さないで下さい。
- b. 実際，私達は彼らが来てくれることを望んでいます。
- c. レセプションホールの収容力は坐席が200人分です。

参考 count out「数に入れない，仲間に入れない，故意に省く」
　　 count in「数に入れる，仲間に入れる，計算に含める」

105.   **c**

訳 新しいマネージャーの名前はなぜまだ発表されていないのですか。
- a. 20人以上のマネージャーが昇進しました。
- b. 全くあなたと同意見です。
- c. 全ては次会の重役会の決定によります。

参考 b は必須表現。be subject to「～による」

106.

When are we supposed to land?

    a. Within about 40 minutes.

    b. In New York.

    c. I suppose we could wait.

107.

Weren't you going to stop delivery on the extra materials?

    a. I'm waiting to hear from the production department.

    b. We don't need any extra materials.

    c. The biggest problem is that our retailers are overstocked right now.

108.

I thought they were supposed to finalize the proposal ASAP?

    a. Yes, but all the necessary figures aren't ready.

    b. Yes, because the final authority rests with the head of finance.

    c. Yes, she's been working on that proposal for three weeks.

109.

Could you order some more ink cartridges for the printer?

    a. The stationary store is closed for the week. We'll have to wait till Monday.

    b. I haven't printed anything for a week, so I don't know.

    c. An order was placed for the printer two days ago.

110.

What do you think of the new assistant manager?

    a. She's been with the company for three years.

    b. I've seen better.

    c. I don't know who has the qualifications.

	解答

106. 基礎知識問題 　　　　　　　　　　　　　　　　　a

訳 いつ，着陸することになっているのですか。
- a. 約40分以内です。
- b. ニューヨークで。
- c. 待てると思います。

参考 Whenの質問に対しては，何らかの方法で時が答えられる。

107. 　　　　　　　　　　　　　　　　　　　　　　　a

訳 余分な材料の配達を止めるのではなかったのですか。
- a. 私は製造部からの知らせを待っている。
- b. 余分な材料は全然必要ではありません。
- c. 一番の問題は現在ストック過剰の小売業者がいるということです。

参考 b は Yes, but I'm waiting to ～ と考えることができる。

108. 　　　　　　　　　　　　　　　　　　　　　　　a

訳 彼らが至急提案を完成させることになっていたと思いますが。
- a. はい。ですが必要な数字が全てそろっているとは言えないのです。
- b. はい。最終的な権限が財務長にあるからです。
- c. はい。彼女はその提案に3週間もかかっています。

参考 ASAP＝as soon as possible　b は質問に対する理由にはならない。

109. 基礎知識問題 　　　　　　　　　　　　　　　　　a

訳 プリンター用のインク・カートリッジをもう少し注文してもらえますか。
- a. 文具店は今週の営業は終わっていますから，月曜日まで待たなければなりません。
- b. 1週間何も印刷してませんから，知りません。
- c. 2日前にプリンターを注文しました。

参考 place an order for 「～を注文する」place an order with 人 for 物

110. 　　　　　　　　　　　　　　　　　　　　　　　b

訳 新しい課長補佐をどう思いますか。
- a. 彼女は会社に3年間勤めています。
- b. もっといい人を知っています。
- c. 誰が資格を持っているのかは知りません。

参考 印象を尋ねるのには How do you like～ もあります。

111.

Where can I buy some baseball equipment?

    a. You can't buy it at the stadium.

    b. Yes, we carry clubs, balls, bags, and tees.

    c. In almost any sporting goods store.

112.

Are they thinking about expanding our product line?

    a. I just found out yesterday.

    b. That's one of the items on today's agenda.

    c. Management never told labor anything until the last minute.

113.

They say the new subway cuts down on travel time. Is that true?

    a. I travel on the subway every day.

    b. It certainly cuts mine down by half.

    c. Now, my commute takes about 35 minutes.

114.

Can you represent our section at the next department meeting?

    a. Our section has given a presentation.

    b. Yes, those department meetings do take a long time.

    c. I'm afraid not. I have to attend a farewell party.

115.

May I get you something to drink, or would you prefer some snacks?

    a. That's OK. I'm fine.

    b. Yes, it would be fine.

    c. Actually, he's trying to cut down on calories.

111. 基礎知識問題   c

訳 野球の装具はどこで買えますか。
  a. スタジアムでは買えません。
  b. はい、私たちはクラブ、ボール、バッグ、そしてティーを扱っています。
  c. ほとんど全てのスポーツ用品店で。

参考 equipment は不可算名詞であり、it で受けます。

112.   b

訳 彼らは我々の製品ラインを広げることを考えているのですか。
  a. 昨日、知ったところです。
  b. それは今日の議題の一つです。
  c. 経営陣は労働者たちには最後の瞬間まで絶対に何も話しませんでした。

参考 現在考慮していることを尋ねています。全選択肢を聴いて判断。

113. 基礎知識問題   b

訳 新しい地下鉄が移動時間を減らすそうですね。
  a. 私は毎日地下鉄に乗ります。
  b. 私の通勤時間も本当に半分になりました。
  c. 現在私の通勤時間は約35分です。

参考 cut down on ~「~を減らす」

114. 基礎知識問題   c

訳 あなたは次の部署会議で我々の部署代表になれますか。
  a. 私の課はプレゼンテーションを行いました。
  b. はい、部署会議は本当に時間がかかります。
  c. 残念ですが、私はお別れパーティーに出席しなければなりません。

参考 Can you に対して No と言わずに I'm afraid not と断わっている。

115. 基礎知識問題   a

訳 何か飲み物をお持ちしましょうか、それとも、スナックがいいですか。
  a. いいえ。おかまいなく。
  b. はい、天気がよいです。
  c. 実際、彼はカロリーの摂取を減らそうとしています。

参考 a は No thank you. I'm fine. に置き換えることもできます。

116.

Our two major competitors are considering a merger, aren't they?

    a. Most of our competitors aren't very eager.

    b. Some people are talking about it, but I'm not sure.

    c. Mergers have become very common in our industry.

117.

How can we persuade our shareholders about the merits of this deal?

    a. The shareholders don't know anything about it.

    b. I read about it in the company newsletter.

    c. It's not going to be easy.

118.

When is Ms. Wu supposed to make the announcement?

    a. At the next regional supervisors' meeting.

    b. Hopefully for only about 45 minutes.

    c. She hasn't checked her manuscript yet.

119.

Did Mr. Singh call while I was out?

    a. Yes, but your colleagues were out.

    b. No, but you have a fax from him on your desk.

    c. Right. He usually calls on the first day of the week.

120.

Who was hired as the systems engineer?

    a. A women with an MBA from Cal.Tech.

    b. The head of the computer department hired her.

    c. I can't say. It's not up to me.

116.   b
訳 我々の主要ライバル2社は合併を考慮しているのですよね。
　　a. ほとんどのライバルは，あまり熱心ではありません。
　　b. そう話している人もいますが，確かではありません。
　　c. 我々の業界では合併が普通になってきました。

参考 c は事実を述べているだけで，疑問に対する回答になっていない。

117.   c
訳 この取引のメリットについてどうやって株主に説得できるでしょうか。
　　a. 株主達はそれについて何も知りません。　　b. それに関しては会社のニュースレターで読みました。　　c. それは簡単ではありません。

参考 主な応答となりうるのは:「説得の方法を述べる」，「わからない」，「説得はできない」というものです。

118.   a
訳 いつウーさんはその告知を行う事になっているのですか。
　　a. 次の地区のスーパーバイザーミーティングで。
　　b. 願わくは45分位だけ。
　　c. 彼女はまだ原稿をチェックしていません。

参考 b は How long に対する応答。

119. 基礎知識問題   b
訳 私が外出している間にシン氏から電話がありましたか。
　　a. はい。でも，あなたの同僚たちは外出していました。
　　b. いいえ。でも，あなたの机の上に彼から来たファックスがあります。
　　c. そうです。彼は大抵，週の最初の日に訪ねてきます。

参考 colleague「同僚」

120. 基礎知識問題   a
訳 システム・エンジニアとして誰が雇われたのですか。
　　a. カリフォルニア工科大でMBAを取得した女性です。
　　b. コンピューター部の部長が彼女を雇いました。
　　c. 言えません。それは私次第ではありません。

参考 MBA = Master of Business Administration「経済学修士」

Part II 応答問題　107

121.

Do you want to rent an apartment in town or buy a house in the suburbs?

    a. Let's buy if we can get a reasonable loan from the bank.
    b. A town house would be nice.
    c. Well, my new office is in the city.

122.

Wouldn't it be better to wait for the sales staff before we begin?

    a. We've waited for them before.
    b. I attended another meeting at three.
    c. Yes, let's do that.

123.

How can you possibly finish that report by tomorrow afternoon?

    a. Yes, I'll start right away.
    b. I guess I'll have to work all night.
    c. I'll probably walk home.

124.

Do you have any plans for your next vacation?

    a. My next vacation isn't until March.
    b. We're going to tour around Europe.
    c. Paris is a beautiful city.

125.

How do we get to the theater?

    a. It's about 10 minutes.
    b. By the time it starts.
    c. It's only three blocks. Let's walk.

121.　　　　　　　　　　　　　　　　　　　　　　　　a

訳　あなたは町でアパートを借りたいですか，それとも郊外に家を買いたいですか。
　　a. 銀行から手ごろなローンを借りられれば買いましょう。　b. タウンハウスがいいですね。　c. ええと，私の新しいオフィスは市内にあります。

参考　or を使用した長い文章ですが，応答の可能性は「2つのうちの1つを選ぶ」「どちらも選ばない」「新しい選択肢を提案する」「わからない」の4つのパターンが考えらます。

122.　　　　　　　　　　　　　　　　　　　　　　　　c

訳　販売スタッフを待って，始めるのが良いのではありませんか。
　　a. 以前に彼らを待ちました。
　　b. 3時にもう1つのミーティングに出席しました。
　　c. はい。そうしましょう。

参考　否定疑問文の情報処理を正しく行えるかが試されています。

123.　　　　　　　　　　　　　　　　　　　　　　　　b

訳　一体どうやって明日の午後までにあのレポートを終えられるのですか。
　　a. はい。すぐに始めます。
　　b. 一晩中がんばらなくてはならないでしょう。
　　c. 私は多分，歩いて家に帰ります。

参考　How は方法，手段，様子，程度など尋ねるときに使う。

124.　　　　　　　　　　　　　　　　　　　　　　　　b

訳　次の休暇の計画は立ててありますか。
　　a. 私の次の休暇は3月までありません。
　　b. 私たちはヨーロッパの色々な所を旅行するつもりです。
　　c. パリは美しい都市です。

参考　a は When is your vacation? に対する応答です。

125.　基礎知識問題　　　　　　　　　　　　　　　　　c

訳　どうやって，劇場に行くのですか。
　　a. およそ10分です。
　　b. それが始まるまでに。
　　c. ほんの3ブロック先です。歩きましょう。

参考　by train, subway, taxi, bus などの表現も再度チェックしよう。

Part II 応答問題　109

126.
Would you like coffee or tea now, or after your meal?
- a. I'd like to get something to drink.
- b. Could you bring me some tea now, please?
- c. Yes, but they both keep me from sleeping.

127.
Are there enough armchairs for the conference?
- a. No, but we have plenty of stackable chairs though.
- b. This time we only have about 30 participants.
- c. Only if they arrived early.

128.
Why don't you ride home with me?
- a. I think I lost my car keys at the gym.
- b. I'm not sure. I have to go straight home tonight.
- c. Good idea. I'll catch up with you in the parking lot.

129.
When should I give Ed the blueprints?
- a. What, you still have them? You should have given them to him yesterday.
- b. How can I trust you? Those blueprints are very important.
- c. When you're finished, have Ed call you.

130.
Don't you think your new office is rather noisy?
- a. It's not what you think, compared to my old one.
- b. No, it's usually very quiet.
- c. No, I don't think anyone here is nosy.

	解答

126.   b

訳 今, コーヒーか紅茶にしますか, それとも食後がいいですか。
   a. 何か飲み物が欲しいです。
   b. 紅茶を今持ってきていだだけますか。
   c. はい。しかしそれらのおかげで寝られなくなります。

参考 or を含んだ疑問文。コーヒーか紅茶を選び, 今か後を指定する。

127.   a

訳 会議用に肘掛け椅子は十分ありますか。
   a. いいえ。でも, 積み重ねのできる椅子なら十分あります。
   b. 今回の参加者は30人くらいだけです。
   c. 彼らが早く着いてくれたらいいのになあ。

参考 c は仮定法過去　If only = I wish

128. 基礎知識問題   c

訳 いっしょに乗って帰りませんか。
   a. 私は私の車のキーをジムで紛失したのだと思います。
   b. 確かではありません。今夜は家にまっすぐ帰らなければなりません。
   c. いい考えだ。駐車場であなたに追いつきますよ。

参考 catch up with は必須表現

129.   a

訳 いつ, エドに青写真をあげるべきですか。
   a. えっ! まだ持っているのですか。昨日, 彼女にそれらを渡しておくべきだったのですよ。　b. 私はどうしてあなたを信用することができるのです? それらの青写真は非常に重要なのです。
   c. あなたが済んだときに, エドがあなたに電話かけるようにしてください。

参考 you should have given「渡しておくべきだったのに」

130.   b

訳 あなたの新しいオフィスはちょっとうるさいと思いませんか。
   a. それはあなたが考えているようなことではありません。私の古いものと比較すると。　b. いいえ, 普段は非常に静かです。
   c. いいえ, ここの人たちは誰も詮索好きではないと思います。

参考 nosy「詮索好き」

131.
How does she come to work?
- a. By bus.
- b. The same shoes.
- c. By nine a.m. every day.

132.
Have you seen the show at the Newtown Theater?
- a. I think I'll catch it next weekend.
- b. Perhaps I'm going to the movies tonight.
- c. I really don't like show business.

133.
Didn't the company offer Richard a higher position?
- a. High positions are hard to come by.
- b. Yes, but he didn't take it.
- c. No, but it can't rise any higher.

134.
Why was this hotel chosen for the conference?
- a. No. There is a very large meeting room.
- b. The conference is always held at a hotel.
- c. Because they gave us better rates than the others.

135.
Who is permitted in the research and development labs?
- a. Only the technicians and specialists.
- b. ID badges are issued to all employees.
- c. The security department gives permission.

131. 基礎知識問題　　　　　　　　　　　　　　　a
訳　彼女はどうやって仕事場にやってくるのですか。
- a. バスで。
- b. 同じ靴。
- c. 毎日9時までに。

132. 基礎知識問題　　　　　　　　　　　　　　　a
訳　ニュータウン劇場でショーを見ましたか。
- a. 来週末それを見ようと思います。
- b. 多分今夜，映画へ行きます。
- c. ショービジネスは全然好きではないのです。

参考　catch「映画・番組を見る」

133.　　　　　　　　　　　　　　　　　　　　　b
訳　会社はリチャードにもっと高い地位を提供しなかったのですか。
- a. 高い地位は手に入れるのが難しいです。
- b. はい。(提供しましたが) 彼は承諾しませんでした。
- c. いいえ。でも，それはこれ以上上昇できません。

参考　come by「手に入る」　rise「上る」

134. 基礎知識問題　　　　　　　　　　　　　　　c
訳　どうしてこのホテルが会議場として選ばれたのですか。
- a. いいえ。非常に大きな会議室があります。
- b. 会議は常にホテルで開催されます。
- c. 他より安い料金をだしてくれたからです。

参考　rate「料金」

135.　　　　　　　　　　　　　　　　　　　　　a
訳　研究開発室へ入る許可をもらえるのは誰ですか。
- a. 技術者と専門家だけです。
- b. IDバッジが全ての従業員に支給されます。
- c. 警備保障部が許可を出します。

参考　issue「発行する」

136.
Isn't the next budget meeting on November 10th?
- a. The new budget hasn't been approved yet.
- b. According to my calendar, it's on November 11th.
- c. Yes, it will be sometime this summer.

137.
Where do you usually buy your ties?
- a. My wife usually advises me.
- b. Usually I get silk, but sometimes I get wool or cotton.
- c. There's a good men's store in the lobby of this building.

138.
Can I use the copier, or is it out of order again?
- a. I asked you not to copy any of my orders.
- b. It's broken for the third time this week.
- c. We ordered coffee but haven't been served yet.

139.
Why don't we go over the figures?
- a. All right. Is sometime this afternoon OK?
- b. The last figures were way over budget.
- c. I can't figure it out. It's too difficult.

140.
Is there a key for this anywhere?
- a. Try Mr. Corazon's top drawer.
- b. I locked it last night.
- c. Any place I look is the same.

解答

136.　　　　　　　　　　　　　　　　　　　　b
|訳| 次の予算会議は11月10日ではないのでか。
　a. 新しい予算はまだ承認されていません。
　b. 私のカレンダーによると11月11日です。
　c. はい。この夏のいつかです。

|参考| ついでに projection「予測」tentative budget「暫定予算」も覚えよう。

137. 基礎知識問題　　　　　　　　　　　　　c
|訳| いつもはどこでネクタイを買うのですか。
　a. 普通は妻が私にアドバイスしてくれます。
　b. 大抵, 絹を買いますが時々はウールか綿を買います。
　c. この建物のロビーに良い紳士用品店があるのです。

|参考| where に対する応答は場所名で答える。

138. 基礎知識問題　　　　　　　　　　　　　b
|訳| コピー機は使えますか, それともまた故障しているのですか。
　a. 私の命令をコピーしないようにあなたに頼みました。
　b. 故障していますよ。今週は3度目ですよ。
　c. 私たちはコーヒーを注文しましたが, まだ来てません。

|参考| コピーやプリンター関係の問題は頻出。表現をチェックする事。

139 基礎知識問題　　　　　　　　　　　　　a
|訳| 数字を調べ直してみませんか。
　a. いいですよ, 今日の午後のいつかでいいですか。
　b. 最後の数字は予算をはるかにオーバーしていました。
　c. 私にはわかりません, 難しい過ぎます。

|参考| go over the figures は必須表現

140. 基礎知識問題　　　　　　　　　　　　　a
|訳| どこかにこれのキーがありますか。
　a. コラゾン氏の一番上の引出しの中を見てください。
　b. 昨晩, それをロックしました。
　c. 見るとどこも同じです。

|参考| top drawer「一番上の引出し」　bottom drawer「一番下の引出し」

Part III 会話問題の攻略法

A フォーマット

　　Part IIIは会話問題で問題数は30です。問題用紙に設問と4つの選択肢があります。それらに目を通しておき，対話を聞いて設問に対する正しい答えの記号を解答用紙にマークします。なお設問と選択肢は放送されません。

B 問題の提示

　　Part IIIの指示文（例題と解答例の提示はありません。）35秒
　　　↓
　　問題開始　Question number 51.（2秒）
　　人物Aのコメント（A1）
　　　↓
　　人物Bの応答（B）
　　　↓
　　人物Aの応答（A2）（A1+B+A2の会話時間　約12秒）
　　　↓（解答用ポーズ　9秒）
　　次の問題開始　Question number 52

C 解答のコツ

　　他のパートと同様に正しいものだと確信できるものには○，そうでないものには×を，その可能性のあるものには△を付けて解答を決定します。Part IIが終わったらすぐに Part III の設問を読み，放送に備えます。放送された語句がそのまま書かれている選択肢は誤答の場合が多いので，自信がないときは選択しないほうがよいでしょう。

D 傾向と対策

　人物A1-人物B-人物A2という構成の会話の流れつかむことが重要ですが，これを聞く前に設問をどれだけ読めるかどうかで対策は二つに分かれます。

　放送に追いつかれてしまう理由の一つは，設問または選択肢が長いときそれを読んで瞬時に理解できないことが挙げられます。少しセンテンスが長めの会話教材を口頭練習することも必要です。選択肢のほとんどは単語か短いフレーズで，センテンスのものは5～8題です。文章の長さはほとんどが10語弱です。

◆ 10問以内に放送に追いつかれてしまう人 ◆

　速読練習が必要です。TOEICスコアが470点以下の場合は問題集で語彙のチェックと場面設定の会話基本パターンの音読とシャドウィングを行います。Part IIIがウィーク・ポイントの場合は，設問のみを読んで解答を推測する練習もします。

　TOEICスコアが470点以上の場合は問題集に頼らず英語ニュースやビデオ教材を利用して視聴覚の両方に訴える体感学習をします。会話を聞いた瞬間に状況判断ができ，その内容がどのように流れるかを予測しながら聞く練習をします。前文の内容を打ち消してしまうような表現や接続詞は特に注意を払って下さい。

◆ Part III が一番苦手な人 ◆

　人物Aと人物Bの会話が速いので話の内容がうまくインプットできないと感じますか。まず練習問題をやってみて，正解しなかった問題のスクリプトを読み，なぜだめだったのかを分析してみましょう。

1. 表現または語彙を知らなかった。
2. 構文・文法的に何を言っているのかわからなかった。
3. スピードが速すぎた。
4. ほとんど知っている語なのにうまく聞き取れなかった。
5. 内容が保持できない。
6. 上記項目のコンビネーション

　第1章のウィーク・ポイントの分析を参照し，一番の弱点を強化することを目指してリスニングのトレーニング・メニューを作成して下さい。テープを使用する場合は音声のスピードがTOEICのPart IIIと同じくらいのものにします。

■ 設問パターン別出題数

what	6~8 題くらい	who	5~6 題くらい
when	4~5 題くらい	where	5 題くらい
why	4~5 題くらい	how	3~5 題くらい

(1) 一般的な設問
1. Who is the man?　注意! 職業を答える。
2. Where is the conversation taking place?
3. What are they talking about?
4. What are they?　注意! 職業を答える。
5. What are they doing?
6. Who are the speakers?　注意! 二人の関係を答える。

(2) 詳細に関する設問
1. When will they meet?
2. What time does the meeting start?
3. How often does he go to the post office?
4. How long was the flight?
5. How will they go to the factory?　注意! 手段を答える。
6. What does he want to do?
7. What is the man suggesting?
8. What is the problem?
9. What is the woman's opinion?
10. What is wrong with the machine?
11. Why did he call?
12. How does the man feel?

(3) 推測する設問
1. What is probably true about~?
2. Who is the woman most likely to meet?

■問題文構成の分析

設問を読んで，放送される会話文のどの部分に注意を払って聞けばよいか予測します。会話の構成パターンを観察し，対策を練ってみましょう。このパートの構文は高校のテキストに出てくる程度のものですが，語彙がビジネス英語中心になっています。出題はダイアローグ形式で，受験者は二人の人物の会話を側で聞いているという設定です。会話のパターンは大きく二つに分類できます。

第1パターン
人物A1のコメントまたは質問—人物Bのコメント—人物A2のコメント

第2パターン
人物A1のコメント — 人物Bコメントまたは質問—人物A2のコメント

第1パターン

タイプ1　人物A1が質問 — 人物Bの応答にキー。
人物A1「疑問文」
↓ Do you have anything to declare?
人物B「疑問に対する答え」正解となるポイントを含む。
↓ I have three bottles of whisky and two watches.
人物A2「通常の応答文」
Oh, it's OK. Please go ahead.
設問　Where does this conversation take place?

タイプ2　人物A1がコメント — 人物Bの応答にキー。
人物A1「通常の文章」
↓ I need to get a new desk.
人物B「通常の応答文」正解となるポイントを含む。
↓ Go to the furniture store by the post office. They're having a sale.
人物A2「一般的応答文」
Great. I can run there during my lunch break.
設問　Where does the man go?

　実際の試験ではこの第1パターン，つまり人物Bの応答に正解のキーがある場合が15題ほどあります。Part IIIの約半分は人物Bのコメントを聞いていれば正解が見つけられるということになります。

第2パターン

　　タイプ1　人物Bが質問 ― 人物A2の応答中にキー。
　　　　人物A1「通常の文章」
　　　　　↓　I have to go to Boston next week.
　　　　人物B　「疑問文」
　　　　　↓　Are you driving or flying?
　　　　人物A2「疑問に対する答え」　正解となるポイントを含む。
　　　　　　　Neither. I'm going to use train this time.
　　　　設問　How will this person go to Boston?

　　タイプ2　人物Bがコメント ― 人物A2の応答中にキー。
　　　　人物A1「通常の文章」
　　　　　↓　George, I want to talk to you about our sales campaign next week.
　　　　人物B　「一般的応答文」
　　　　　↓　Well, I have nothing scheduled on Tuesday and Wednesday.
　　　　人物A2「通常の応答文」正解となるポイントを含む。
　　　　　　　Wednesday is most convenient for me.
　　　　設問　When will they meet?

　　このパターンは合わせて8〜10問ではないかと思われます。特に，どこかに行くための交通手段や会議の時間を問うものなどが典型的なものです。
　　　　　　How does he go to Los Angeles?
　　　　　　　By car.　By bus.　By train.　By plane.
　　　　　　When will they meet?
　　　　　　　Monday.　Tuesday.　Wednesday.
　　　　　　What time will they leave?
　　　　　　　At 9:00 a.m.　At 10:00 a.m.

第3パターン
全体を聞いて推測し、判断する問題　2〜3題
　　人物 A1「通常の文章」
　　　↓　Here are your air tickets and hotel vouchers.
　　人物 B「通常の文章」
　　　↓　Thank you, Jeff. Could you book the night tour for me?
　　人物 A2「通常の応答文」
　　　　Sure. The tour bus will pick you up at your hotel
　　　　at 7:00 p.m.
　　設問　Who is Jeff?

　　　話者の職業や、話者同士の関係や会話の行われている場所などに関する問題が考えられます。
　　　　　Where does this conversation take place?
　　　　　　　At a realtor's office.
　　　　　Who are the speakers?
　　　　　　　A clerk and a customer.
　　　　　　　A waitress and a customer.

第4パターン
人物A1のコメント中にキー。1〜2題
　　人物 A1「通常の文章」正解となるポイントを含む。
　　　↓　Let's rewrite the contract draft tomorrow.
　　人物 B「通常の応答文」
　　　↓　That's fine with me. I want to go over each of the
　　　　articles tonight.
　　人物 A2「一般的応答文」
　　　　So do I. Well, I'll see you in room 201 as usual, then.
　　設問　What will they do tomorrow?

　　　人物A1が冒頭で自分が何を行いたいのかを述べます。その後話が展開しますが、問題は詳細についてのものではなく「何をしたいのか」や「何を買いたいのか」などが問われます。概要を覚えておく練習も必要です。
　　　　　What does the man want to do?
　　　　　　　Cash his check.　Borrow some money.

Part III　会話問題　　121

リスニング Part III　頻出英単語

accept	受け入れる	advertise	広告する
afford	余裕を持つ	announce	発表する
argue	議論する	attend	出席する
be available	利用できる	be promoted	昇進する
be upset	動転する，怒る	cancel	キャンセルする
complete	完成する	conserve	保存する
cut down on	〜を減らす	delay	遅れる
deliver	配達する	deposit	預ける
describe	描写する	distribute	配布する
develop	発展する，現像する	enlarge	拡大する
expect	予期する	extend	延長する，拡張する
forfeit	失う，没収される	go over	よく調べる，手直しする
go through	検討する，体験する	guarantee	保証する
happen	起こる	improve	改善する
increase	増加する	install	インストールする
interview	面接する	invest	投資する
lose one's job	仕事を失う	mention	述べる
order	注文する，命令する	pack	パックする，詰める
package	小包にする	postpone	延期する
proofread	校正する	provide	提供する
receive	受け取る	reduce	減る
rent	賃貸する	repair	修理する
replace	取り替える	request	要請する
resolve	決定する	save	節約する，救う
specify	指定する	spill	こぼす，流出
stretch	伸びる，伸ばす	submit	提出する
suggest	提案する	supervise	監督する
train	訓練する	transfer	乗り換える
wave	振る	weigh	計る

練習問題1－100

会話を聞いて設問を読み，正しい答を選んでください。
（設問と選択肢はできるだけ問題文放送の前に読むこと。）解答→p.140

Part III

1.　　　　　　　　　　　　　　　　　　　2-02
What is she going to buy for him?
- a. Plastic boxes.
- b. Staples.
- c. Some samples.
- d. office supplies.

2.
How is the technician doing?
- a. Adjusting well.
- b. Working hard.
- c. Having a difficult time.
- d. Waiting a few weeks.

3.
What is the man going to do?
- a. Land soon.
- b. Update his résumé.
- c. Meet his secretary.
- d. Read his e-mail.

4.　　　　　　　　　　　　　　　　　　　2-03
Who forgot to deduct the taxes?
- a. Somebody.
- b. Philip.
- c. Ms. Amato.
- d. A manager.

5.
What is she doing?
- a. Repairing the production line.
- b. Drinking coffee.
- c. Running back to the production line again.
- d. Arranging the cases.

6.
What will the shipping department do?
- a. Paint labels.
- b. Mark crates and boxes.
- c. Give instructions.
- d. Complain about customers.

Part III 会話問題

7.   2-04

What is the woman going to do?
- a. Buy him lunch.
- b. Get some make-up.
- c. Give him a box.
- d. Share her lunch.

8.

When are they going to meet?
- a. Wednesday at 12:30.
- b. Tuesday at 11:15.
- c. After brunch at 1:15.
- d. Next Thursday at lunchtime.

9.

Where does this conversation take place?
- a. On a ship.
- b. At a swimming pool.
- c. At a church.
- d. On a beach.

10.   2-05

What are they doing?
- a. Making a shipment.
- b. Checking a contract.
- c. Paying a penalty.
- d. Meeting a condition.

11.

What has the man been promised to do?
- a. Fix a fan.
- b. Buy a new air-conditioner.
- c. Call a custodian.
- d. Turn the fan off.

12.

Who are the speakers?
- a. A mailperson and a secretary.
- b. A salesman and a customer.
- c. A messenger and a clerk.
- d. A programmer and a customer.

13. ——————————— 2-06

What is she doing?
- a. Selling a car.
- b. Driving to her job.
- c. Buying new tires.
- d. Improving her condition.

14.

Where is the conversation taking place?
- a. At customs.
- b. At a boutique.
- c. At a perfumery.
- d. At a department store.

15.

Who is the woman?
- a. A typist.
- b. A teacher.
- c. A writer.
- d. A student.

16. ——————————— 2-07

What is he looking for?
- a. The vice-president's secretary.
- b. A report summary.
- c. A documentary.
- d. The previous year's file.

17.

What is she doing?
- a. Looking for a hospital.
- b. Studying to be an administrator.
- c. Trying to find a book.
- d. Returning a book.

18.

What does she want to do?
- a. Withdraw $50.
- b. Open a bank account.
- c. Ask about the balance.
- d. Obtain $2000.

19. ——————————— 2-08

What are they going to do?
- a. Make a call.
- b. Discuss a proposition.
- c. Talk about a delivery.
- d. Pay a late fee.

20.
What are they talking about?
    a. The woman's qualifications.
    b. Hiring a new employee.
    c. Deciding on the best position.
    d. What to do at the end of the month.

21.
What are they talking about?
    a. The need to pack up their products.
    b. The way that's cheapest.
    c. How to send product samples.
    d. Finding a delivery company.

22.   2-09
What are they discussing?
    a. The amount of inventory.   b. The size of the Chicago store.
    c. The coming holiday season.   d. A discount sale.

23.
What is the man's job?
    a. A bellman.   b. A porter.
    c. A doorman.   d. A front desk clerk.

24.
What are they discussing?
    a. Going to the market.   b. How many shares Lewis bought.
    c. Purchasing stock.   d. A company's financial policy.

25.   2-10
What are they talking about?
    a. Checking the books.   b. Extra hotel charges.
    c. Winter in New Zealand.   d. Additional vacation time.

26.
What is this discussion about?
 a. The quality of the research department.
 b. Expenditure cuts.
 c. The growth rate of the company.
 d. Buying new computers.

27.
What are the man and woman talking about?
 a. Hiring new employees.   b. Improving the packaging system.
 c. The high cost of salaries.   d. Their expertise.

28.   2-11
What is the man's job?
 a. A part-time worker.   b. A schoolteacher.
 c. A convenience store manager.   d. A real estate agent.

29.
What is this conversation about?
 a. Their wrists.   b. Client complaints.
 c. Company records.   d. His assistant's job.

30.
What are they discussing?
 a. Keeping merchandise.   b. The plans for a new building.
 c. The effect of sales.   d. Their competition.

31.   2-12
Who is the man?
 a. A tailor.   b. A shipper.
 c. A trucker.   d. A laundry man.

32.

What's wrong with the taxi?
- a. It's not clean.
- b. It doesn't have an air-conditioner.
- c. It's dangerous.
- d. It smells bad.

33.

What is this conversation about?
- a. Publishing books.
- b. Printing a photo.
- c. The high cost of printing.
- d. Replacing their machinery.

34. — 2-13

What is Steve's problem?
- a. He canceled the meeting.
- b. He can't attend the meeting.
- c. He has to assist his boss.
- d. He couldn't make the summary.

35.

What is their main concern?
- a. The training schedule.
- b. Finding a faster train.
- c. Keeping their appointment.
- d. The weather forecast.

36.

What was Ms. Galvan's problem?
- a. There was an accident on the ship.
- b. Components were lost.
- c. There was an accident at the firm.
- d. The shipment didn't arrive on time.

37. — 2-14

Why is the man upset?
- a. He's afraid of losing his job.
- b. His section is taking the day off.
- c. He made a mistake in calculation.
- d. The manager was fired.

38.
What is the woman's problem?
   a. The price of her stock is going down.
   b. Her order is late.
   c. There was an explosion in the factory.
   d. There wasn't any stationery.

39.
What did the man do?
   a. He got extra electricians.
   b. He rescheduled their project.
   c. He dismissed the sub-contractor.
   d. He had the walls demolished.

40.
2-15

What does the man need to do?
   a. Phone the trucking company.
   b. Notify the truckers.
   c. Mail the invoice.
   d. Check the boxes.

41.
What is the man's problem?
   a. He's late for a meeting.
   b. He can't sign out a car.
   c. It's in her drawer.
   d. They have to make a policy.

42.
What is their problem?
   a. There's too much smoke.
   b. The tables are too close.
   c. It's too noisy.
   d. They can't change tables.

43. ———————————— 2-16

What is his complaint?
- a. He requested a reservation.
- b. The flight is fully booked.
- c. He squeezed too tightly.
- d. He didn't get the seat he wanted.

44.

What is the man's opinion of Ms. Whitney's point?
- a. It's a good idea.
- b. Her timing is way off.
- c. November is OK.
- d. She's very considerate.

45.

What is the woman's profession?
- a. A sub-contractor.
- b. A tennis teacher.
- c. A lawyer.
- d. An executive.

46. ———————————— 2-17

What is the woman's position?
- a. A receptionist.
- b. A reservationist.
- c. An advertising agent.
- d. An answering service employee.

47.

What are their jobs?
- a. Equipment suppliers.
- b. Accountants.
- c. Machine inspectors.
- d. Salespeople.

48.

What is the man's occupation?
- a. A computer programmer.
- b. A desk clerk.
- c. A salesman.
- d. A graphic designer.

49. 2-18

What is this conversation about?
- a. A meeting at the end of the week.
- b. Excessive shipping costs.
- c. The next annual report.
- d. How to transport merchandise.

50.

What is the woman's job?
- a. A technician.
- b. A manager.
- c. A chauffeur.
- d. A public speaker.

51.

What does the woman think about the bonds?
- a. Technology and oil stocks are less risky.
- b. They're fine for the short-term.
- c. They're not good for short-term investment.
- d. It's too late to buy them.

52. 2-19

What does the man think?
- a. The train is economical.
- b. Most people prefer to fly.
- c. It's generally inconvenient.
- d. Many people don't fly.

53.

What does the man think will happen?
- a. He will go along with the market.
- b. The experts will write magazines.
- c. He will think about the contract.
- d. Stock prices will go down.

54.

What is the woman's opinion?
- a. Cut the number of copies.
- b. Limit the number of employees.
- c. Repair the copy machine.
- d. Think about it for a month.

55. 2-20

What did the board think of the report?
- a. It didn't have enough facts.
- b. It wasn't long enough.
- c. He worked for a month.
- d. They liked it well enough.

56.

In the man's opinion, what should the company do?
- a. Get a new law firm.
- b. Employ staff lawyers.
- c. Charge on a yearly basis.
- d. Think about the time.

57.

What is the woman's opinion of Prof. Riseman?
- a. He's not truthful.
- b. He is a knowledgeable teacher.
- c. He exerts himself in the field.
- d. He gives too much homework.

58. 2-21

What does the woman think?
- a. The mid-size frames are too small.
- b. They should buy the stocks now.
- c. The hard drives will be cost effective.
- d. She doubts the specifications.

59.

What does Allan think she should do?
- a. Write to the trucker.
- b. Give the manager a present.
- c. Stop working extra hours.
- d. Say she wants a higher wage.

60.
What is the man's occupation?
- a. A deliveryman.
- b. An architect.
- c. A sales representative.
- d. A shipping clerk.

61. 2-22
What does the man suggest?
- a. To go the customer service section.
- b. To open a commercial account.
- c. To go to the lobby first.
- d. To go to the service station.

62.
When will the antique car show be held?
- a. Over the weekend.
- b. In four weeks.
- c. Next month.
- d. In July.

63.
What is the man's advice?
- a. That she's running in a hurry.
- b. That she leave earlier.
- c. To go next time.
- d. To make sure of the time.

64. 2-23
What does the man suggest?
- a. Hire a skilled agent.
- b. Fire the new office assistant.
- c. Use an employment agency.
- d. Get some qualifications.

65.
What is the woman's advice to the man?
- a. To go to the convention in three days.
- b. To wait until he's sure.
- c. To visit the richest customers only.
- d. To stop at the best customers.

66.

What is her advice?
- a. To cash a payroll check.
- b. To go to a bank.
- c. To check the cash.
- d. To wait on the corner.

67. 2-24

What does the man suggest?
- a. Hire some temporary help.
- b. Give them a hand now.
- c. Finish the balance sheets.
- d. Wait for a week.

68.

Where are they speaking?
- a. On a plane.
- b. At a hotel.
- c. In a bedroom.
- d. In a department store.

69.

What does she suggest?
- a. Gaining weight.
- b. Exercising.
- c. Working less.
- d. Taking more breaks.

70. 2-25

What does she suggest to Tony?
- a. To install some equipment.
- b. To bring his family.
- c. To stay a minimum of a few days.
- d. To telephone his family.

71.

What does she suggest?
- a. He come to her office.
- b. He look at the facilities.
- c. It was nice to meet him.
- d. He join the organization.

72.

Where will they put the coffee maker?
- a. In the lunchroom.
- b. In the employee lounge.
- c. In the shipping department.
- d. On the factory floor.

73.   2-26

Where is the trade show being held?
    a. At the Atlantic Hotel.   b. In a crowded exhibition center.
    c. In Atlanta.   d. In Zurich.

74. Where does this conversation take place?
    a. In front of a restaurant.   b. Near a new office.
    c. Outside a factory.   d. At a park.

75.

Where will the new store probably be located?
    a. Downtown.   b. By the highway.
    c. In the suburbs.   d. Near the train station.

76.   2-27

How long will Sue be in Dallas?
    a. She's not really sure.   b. For three weeks.
    c. It depends if the director likes her.   d. At least a week.

77.

Where does this conversation take place?
    a. In a real estate agency.   b. At a distribution center.
    c. At a service station.   d. At an automobile dealership.

78.

In which department are they speaking?
    a. The tax department.   b. The accounting department.
    c. The personnel department.   d. The production department.

79.   2-28

Where is the report?
    a. By the copier.   b. In the file cabinet.
    c. With the assistant manager.   d. On the coffee machine.

80.
What does Mrs. Kanemoto suggest?
    a. To give the budgets first.
    b. To change the topic order.
    c. To give the presentation next week.
    d. To start production fast.

81.
Where does this conversation take place?
    a. In a rental shop.   b. In a bank.
    c. At a lawyer's office.   d. At a stock broker's office.

82.   2-29
Where are the ski slopes located?
    a. A short trip from Vancouver.   b. Quite near the city.
    c. Close to his children's school.   d. By the manager's office.

83.
How long can the company stay in its present facilities?
    a. Till the manager buys the office.   b. For less than a year.
    c. Until the company stops growing.   d. For the time being.

84.
How much vacation time does a new employee begin with?
    a. Two weeks.   b. Three weeks.
    c. Four weeks.   d. Five weeks.

85.   2-30
At what time does the mail usually come?
    a. Soon.   b. After lunchtime.
    c. At 2:00 p.m.   d. In the morning.

86.
At what time does the meeting start?
- a. At ten minutes to eleven.
- b. At 11:45.
- c. Before she gets any coffee.
- d. When she gets to the factory floor.

87.
When can Sharon meet Jeff?
- a. In a few minutes.
- b. As soon as Frank leaves.
- c. Tomorrow in the law library.
- d. The day after tomorrow.

88.
At what time does she want the limousine?
- a. At exactly 7 o'clock.
- b. At 7:10.
- c. At 7:15.
- d. At 7:45.

89.
Why is the woman working?
- a. So she can go skiing.
- b. Because she missed some days.
- c. So she will be free in two weeks.
- d. Because she had a long vacation.

90.
Why didn't she send the tax figures?
- a. Helen couldn't find the report.
- b. The e-mail system is being revised.
- c. The auditing department opens this afternoon.
- d. They're not finished yet.

91.   2-32

Why will the man be at the office?
    a. He can't spend time with his family.
    b. He now has more responsibilities.
    c. The president doesn't like him.
    d. Because he enjoys doing paperwork.

92.

When are they going to leave for the airport?
    a. By 9:20.   b. At 10 o'clock.
    c. After 12:30.   d. Early.

93.

Why did Mr. Kelly lose his job?
    a. He started a fire in the company.
    b. He was angry at an employee.
    c. An executive didn't like him.
    d. He wasn't a very good worker.

94.   2-33

How often does he play tennis?
    a. Every week.   b. Twice a month.
    c. On the weekends. d. Daily since he was nine years old.

95.

Why couldn't she finish the figures?
    a. Her computer wouldn't function.
    b. It was a rough take-off.
    c. Her PC was not allowed on board.
    d. The flight was too short.

96.

Why is there no monthly report today?
    a. There are some labor problems.
    b. It's not the right day.
    c. It isn't justified yet.
    d. They are buying new equipment.

97.   2-34

Why is her assistant going to the supplier?
    a. To complain about the concrete price of concrete.
    b. To talk to the retired salesman.
    c. For a construction estimate.
    d. To find out who the new representative is.

98.

Why did it take Carlos so long to finish?
    a. He was working on some export papers.
    b. Because he's not strong enough.
    c. He's not an expert in that field.
    d. It took him five hours.

99.   2-35

Why can't the woman make the meeting?
    a. She was ordered not to.   b. She has a lot of paperwork.
    c. Because Bill will take notes.   d. She's going to proceed.

100.

Why is she leaving?
    a. She wants to get home before dark.
    b. Thirty minutes is too long.
    c. She hates parties.
    d. The seminar wasn't so interesting.

Part III Scripts

1.

Woman: Does anybody need anything? I'm going to the stationery store for some staples.

Man: Thanks Ann. Could you pick me up a dozen plastic folders, a box of rubber bands, and some product labels?

Woman: Do you want colored folders or just plain?

Q What is she going to buy for him?

    a. Plastic boxes.   b. Staples.
    c. Some samples.   d. Office supplies.

2.

Man: How is that new technician working out in the R and D department?

Woman: He's having a really hard time. He's just not used to working on a team.

Man: That's too bad. Maybe he needs a few more weeks to adjust.

Q How is the technician doing?

    a. Adjusting well.   b. Working hard.
    c. Having a difficult time.   d. Waiting a few weeks.

3.

Man: As soon as the plane lands, I'm going to plug in my PC and check my e-mail.

Woman: I thought you checked it just before we took off?

Man: I did, but I'm expecting my secretary to send an important update I need for my presentation.

Q What is the man going to do?

    a. Land soon.   b. Update his résumé.
    c. Meet his secretary.   d. Read his e-mail.

スクリプト 訳

1. 基礎知識問題   **d**

訳 女性: 誰か何かいります？ホチキスの針を買いに文房具店に行きますが。
  男性: ありがとうアン，プラスチックのフォルダー1ダース，輪ゴム1箱と製品用のラベルを買ってきてください。
  女性: カラー・フォルダーそれとも無色がいいですか。

Q 彼女は彼に何を買うのですか。
  a. プラスチックの箱   b. ホチキスの針
  c. サンプル数個   d. 事務用品

参考 このタイプの「買い物」問題は，人物A1-人物B-人物A2の会話で人物Bの応答がヒントとなる可能性が大きい。

2.   **c**

訳 男性: 新しい技術者は研究開発部で皆とうまくやれているのかな。
  女性: 全然だめ。彼はチームとして働くことに全く慣れていないのよ。
  男性: 大変だな。多分，慣れるまでにもう2～3週間掛かるかもしれない。

Q 技術者の様子はどうですか。
  a. よく調整している。   b. 一生懸命に働いている。
  c. 苦労している。   d. 2～3週待っている。

参考 人物Bの応答がヒント。R=Research　D=Development

3.   **d**

訳 男性: 着陸したらすぐに，私のパソコンを接続して，Eメールをチェックするぞ。
  女性: 私たちが飛び立つ前にあなたはチェックしたと思っていたわ。
  男性: しましたよ，でも，私のプレゼンテーションで必要な 重要最新情報を秘書が送ってくるのを待っているのです。

Q 男性は何をするのですか。
  a. すぐに着陸する。   b. 彼の履歴を更新する。
  c. 彼の秘書に会う。   d. 彼の電子メールを読む。

参考 update「更新する」

Part III 会話問題

4.

Woman: Philip, have the manager and Ms. Amato from accounting meet me in my office right away.

Man: Sure. What seems to be the problem?

Woman: Someone forgot to deduct the taxes from last month's sales commissions.

Q Who forgot to deduct the taxes?
   a. Somebody.   b. Philip.
   c. Ms. Amato.   d. A manager.

5.

Man: Vera, put that coffee down and get back to work. Your break was over 10 minutes ago.

Woman: I know, but the production line is still down for repairs.

Man: In that case, get back as soon as it's running again.

Q What is she doing?
   a. Repairing the production line.
   b. Drinking coffee.
   c. Running back to the production line again.
   d. Arranging the cases.

6.

Woman: I want every shipment clearly marked and labeled. Our customers have been complaining about delivery problems recently.

Man: How do you want the shipping department to do it?

Woman: Mark all the crates and boxes with large blue signs, and use red paint on the bags.

Q What will the shipping department do?
   a. Paint labels.   b. Mark crates and boxes.
   c. Give instructions.   d. Complain about customers.

4.　基礎知識問題　　　　　　　　　　　　　　　　　　　　a

訳　女性：フィリップ，支配人と会計部のアマートさんに私のオフィスにすぐ来てもらって。
　　男性：いいよ。どうかしたの？
　　女性：誰かが先月の販売の手数料から税金を差し引くのを忘れたのよ。

Q　誰が税金を差し引くのを忘れたのですか。
　a．誰か。　　　　　　　　　　b．フィリップ。
　c．Ms. アマート。　　　　　　d．マネージャー。

参考　deduct「差し引く，控除する」　commission「手数料」

5.　　　　　　　　　　　　　　　　　　　　　　　　　　b

訳　男性：ベラ，コーヒーを置いて仕事に戻ったら？休憩は10分前終わっているよ。
　　女性：わかっているわ。でも生産ラインが修理のために止まっているの。
　　男性：そういうことなら動き始めたらすぐに頼むよ。

Q　彼女は何をしているのですか。
　a．生産ラインを修理している。　　b．コーヒーを飲んでいる。
　c．生産ラインに走って戻って行くところ。　d．ケースを並べている。

参考　人物Aの初めのコメントがヒントになっている。

6.　　　　　　　　　　　　　　　　　　　　　　　　　　b

訳　女性：積荷の全部にはっきりマークして，ラベルもつけてね。最近，お客様達から配達のことで苦情を受けているの。
　　男性：輸送部はどうすればいいのですか。
　　女性：木枠と箱はすべて青で大きく書いて，バッグには赤のペンキを使うようにして。

Q　輸送部は何をするのですか。
　a．ラベルにペンキを塗る。　　　b．木枠と箱にマークを付ける。
　c．指示を与える。　　　　　　　d．顧客について不平を言べる。

参考　label「ラベルをつける」　crate「木枠」

7.

Man: Oh, no! I forgot to bring my lunch box this morning. I'll be starving by quitting time.
Woman: That's OK. You can share mine. I've got plenty.
Man: Thanks, I appreciate it. I'll make it up to you.

Q What is the woman going to do?

    a. Buy him lunch.   b. Get some make-up.
    c. Give him a box.   d. Share her lunch.

8.

Woman: Mark, it's been a long time. Why don't we get together for lunch sometime? How about this Tuesday at 1:15 at Anthony's Cafe?
Man: Sure Pam, Anthony's sounds good. But I can't make it this Tuesday, though anytime Wednesday is fine with me.
Woman: OK, see you at 12:30 then. I'm looking forward to it.

Q When are they going to meet?

    a. Wednesday at 12:30.   b. Tuesday at 11:15.
    c. After brunch at 1:15.   d. Next Thursday at lunchtime.

9.

Woman: This cruise ship is great. It has so many facilities.
Man: I know. I can't wait to take a swim in the pool.
Woman: I'm glad we decided on this for our honeymoon.

Q Where does this conversation take place?

    a. On a ship.   b. At a swimming pool.
    c. At a church.   d. On a beach.

7.

訳 男性: ああいけない。今朝，私の弁当箱を持ってくるのを忘れた。帰る時間までに飢えちゃうよ。
女性: 大丈夫。私のお弁当を分けてあげるわ。
男性: 有難う。心から感謝するよ。埋め合わせするよ。

Q 女性は何をするのですか。
a. 彼に昼食を買ってあげる。 b. メーキャップを手に入れる。
c. 彼に箱を与える。 d. 彼女の昼食を分けてあげる。

解答 d

参考 make up「埋め合わせをする」

8. 基礎知識問題

訳 女性: マーク，しばらく。いつかいっしょに昼食でもどう？今週の火曜日にアンソニーのカフェで1時15分というのはどうかしら？
男性: いいよパム。アンソニーはいいね。でも今週の火曜日はだめなんだ。水曜日なら何時でもいいのだけれど。
女性: OK。では水曜の12時半に。楽しみにしているわ。

Q 彼らはいつ会うのですか。
a. 水曜日の12時30分。 b. 火曜日の11時15分。
c. ブランチの後1時15分。 d. 次の木曜日の昼食時。

解答 a

参考 時間と曜日の組み合わせ問題はこのパターンが基本。

9.

訳 女性: このクルーザーはすばらしいわね。設備がすごく充実しているわ。
男性: そうだね。私はプールで泳ぐのが待ち切れないよ。
女性: 新婚旅行をこれに決めてうれしいわ。

Q この会話はどこで交わされていますか。
a. 船上。 b. プールで。
c. 教会で。 d. 海岸で。

解答 a

参考 クルーザーの設備の話をしているところから，二人が新婚旅行中で，すでに船上にいると推測できる。

Part III 会話問題

10.

    Man: The second paragraph requires us to have the shipment at their plant by March 14th.
Woman: That's a difficult condition. What if we can't meet it?
    Man: The next paragraph says that we have to pay a late penalty for each additional day.

Q What are they doing?

    a. Making a shipment.   b. Checking a contract.
    c. Paying a penalty.   d. Meeting a condition.

11.

Woman: The heat is too high in here and the fan is really loud.
    Man: OK, I'll call maintenance and have someone take care of it right away.
Woman: Thanks. I appreciate it. It's really hard to concentrate under these conditions.

Q What has the man promised to do?

    a. Fix a fan.   b. Buy a new air-conditioner.
    c. Call a custodian.   d. Turn the fan off.

12.

    Man: I'd like it set up so that my e-mail notification automatically comes on, when I turn the computer on.
Woman: Do you want an audio signal, too?
    Man: No, just the flashing message box will be fine.

Q Who are the speakers?

    a. A mailperson and a secretary.
    b. A salesman and a customer.
    c. A messenger and a clerk.
    d. A programmer and a customer.

解答

10. b

訳 男性: 第2項によると，3月14日までに荷を先方の工場に届けなければならない。
女性: 難しい条件ね。もしそれが満たせない場合はどうなのですか。
男性: 次の項によると遅滞は日割で，罰金を支払わなければならないとなっている。

Q 彼らは何をしているのですか。
　a. 出荷している。　　　　　b. 契約をチェックしている。
　c. 罰金を払っている。　　　d. 条件を満たしている。

参考 paragraph「(契約の)項」

11. c

訳 女性: ここは暑すぎるし，扇風機の音がすごく大きいわね。
男性: OK，メンテナンスに電話してすぐ誰かにどうにかしてもらうよ。
女性: 有難う，感謝するわ。こんな状況では集中するのに苦労するわ。

Q 男性は何をする約束をしましたか。
　a. 扇風機を直す。　　　　　b. 新しいエアコンを買う。
　c. 管理人を呼ぶ。　　　　　d. 扇風機を止める。

参考 maintenance man「保守管理者」　custodian「管理人」
　　 janitor「管理人」

12. d

訳 男性: スイッチを入れた時に，電子メールの通知が自動的に入るようにセットアップしてもらいたいのです。
女性: 音声の信号もセットします？
男性: いえ，光が点いたり消えたりするメッセージ・ボックスだけでいいです。

Q 誰が話しているのですか。
　a. 郵便配達人と秘書。　　　b. セールスマンと客。
　c. メッセンジャーと書記。　d. プログラマーと客。

参考 set up, message box などのコンピューター関係語彙は要注意。

Part III 会話問題　147

13.

Woman: It only has 25,000 miles on it, and the tires are all new.

Man: It looks like it's in good condition. How long have you had it?

Woman: For about two years. I mostly just drove it to my job over at Allied Industries.

Q What is she doing?

    a. Selling a car.   b. Driving to her job.

    c. Buying new tires.   d. Improving her condition.

14.

Man: Good afternoon Ma'am. Could you please open that small suitcase?

Woman: Of course. There're only a few clothes in it.

Man: I see you have three new bottles of perfume. How much did they cost?

Q Where is the conversation taking place?

    a. At customs.   b. At a boutique.

    c. At a perfumery.   d. At a department store.

15.

Woman: For next week, please read chapter seven and write a short report.

Man: Is it OK to write it by hand, or do you want it typed?

Woman: I'd rather it was typed, but if that's not possible, go ahead and write it out.

Q Who is the woman?

    a. A typist.   b. A teacher.

    c. A writer.   d. A student.

解答

13.   a

訳 女性: 走行距離は25,000マイルだけです。しかもタイヤは全部新品です。
　　男性: 良い状態のようですね。手に入れてどのくらいになるのですか。
　　女性: 2年くらいです。大体は私の仕事場のAllied Industries社に行くのに運転しただけです。

Q 彼女は何をしているのですか。
　a. 車を売っている。　　　　　　b. 彼女の仕事に運転していく。
　c. 新しいタイヤを買っている。　d. 彼女の状況を改善している。

参考 女性が自分の車を中古車ディーラーに売っていることに気付けるかどうかがポイント。

14.   a

訳 男性: こんにちは、奥様。その小さいスーツケースを開けてください。
　　女性: はい。服が三着入っているだけです。
　　男性: 新しい香水を3本お持ちですね、いくらでしたか。

Q この会話はどこで交わされているのですか。
　a. 税関。　　　　　　b. ブティック。
　c. 香水製造所。　　　d. デパート。

参考 customs official「税管吏」との会話です。　customs duty「関税」
immigration「入国管理」　declare「申告する」

15.   b

訳 女性: 来週に関しては、第7章を読み、短いレポートを書いてください。
　　男性: それは、手書きでいいですか、それともタイプ書きが良いですか。
　　女性: タイプだといいですね。でも、無理だったら気兼ねなく手書きにしてください。

Q 女性の職業は何ですか。
　a. タイピスト。　　　　b. 先生。
　c. 作家。　　　　　　　d. 学生。

参考 冒頭の言葉で女性が教師であると推測できる。

16.

Woman: Armando, did you find the summary of this year's operating expense report?
Man: I've been looking all morning, but I still can't find it.
Woman: Try last year's files. If it's not there, ask the vice-president's secretary.

Q What is he looking for?

a. The vice-president's secretary.
b. A report summary.
c. A documentary.
d. The previous year's file.

17.

Man: Yes, we have a complete management section. Are you looking for a particular subject?
Woman: Yes, something on hospital administration.
Man: Try the bottom left shelf in Aisle 5.

Q What is she doing?

a. Looking for a hospital.
b. Studying to be an administrator.
c. Trying to find a book.
d. Returning a book.

18.

Woman: Excuse me, but could you tell me the minimum deposit to open an account?
Man: Yes, it's fifty dollars, but you must maintain a balance of two hundred dollars or there is a three-dollar monthly charge.
Woman: I see. In that case, I'd like to deposit two thousand dollars.

Q What does she want to do?

a. Withdraw $50.
b. Open a bank account.
c. Ask about the balance.
d. Obtain $2000.

16.   b

[訳] 女性: アーマンド，今年の営業費報告の要約はありましたか。
男性: 午前中ずっと探しているのですが，まだ見つけていません。
女性: 去年のファイルをご覧になって，もしそこになければ副社長の秘書に聞いてご覧なさい。

[Q] 彼は何を捜しているのですか。
a. 副社長の秘書。　　　　　　b. 統括報告。
c. ドキュメンタリー。　　　　d. 前年度のファイル。

[参考] summary「要約」（summary report 概略報告）（report summary 統括報告）operating expense「営業経費，運用費」

17.   c

[訳] 男性: はい，「管理関係」の充実したセクションがあります。何か特定のテーマで捜しているのですか。
女性: はい。病院管理に関するものを探しています。
男性: 通路5の棚の下段左を見てください。

[Q] 彼女は何をしているのですか。
a. 病院を捜している。　　　　b. 管理者になるために勉強している。
c. 本を探しいる。　　　　　　d. 本を返している。

[参考] 管理者になるための勉強をしているかは定かでないのでbは除外する。

18.   b

[訳] 女性: すみませんが，口座を開設するのに必要な最小金額はどのくらいですか。
男性: はい，50ドルですが200ドルの残高を維持しない場合，月に3ドルの手数料が掛かります。
女性: わかりました。それでは2000ドルを預金したいと思います。

[Q] 彼女は何をしたいのですか。
a. 50ドル引き出す。　　　　　b. 銀行口座を開く。
c. 残高について尋ねる。　　　d. 2000ドルを得る。

[参考] deposit「預金する」　withdraw「引き出す」　interest「利子」

Part III 会話問題

19.

Man: I think it's a pretty good deal. If we can deliver two months early we get an 8% bonus.
Woman: That's right. But don't forget, if we can't meet the deadline we have to pay a late fee.
Man: Well, I think we should call right away and let them know we accept.

Q What are they going to do?

   a. Make a call.   b. Discuss a proposition.
   c. Talk about a delivery.   d. Pay a late fee.

20.

Woman: Have you read through all the applications yet?
Man: Yes, I have, but it's difficult to come to a decision. They all seem to be very well qualified.
Woman: Well, the position has to be filled by the end of the month, so we'll have to decide as soon as possible.

Q What are they talking about?

   a. The woman's qualifications. b. Hiring a new employee.
   c. Deciding on the best position. d. What to do at the end of the month.

21.

Woman: Which do you think is the most efficient way to send out these samples?
Man: A package delivery company would be the fastest, but regular mail would be the cheapest, even though it will take about a week longer.
Woman: Let's go with the delivery company. It's important that our customers get them as quick as possible.

Q What are they talking about?

   a. The need to pack up their products.
   b. The way that's cheapest.
   c. How to send product samples.
   d. Finding a delivery company.

解答

19. 　　　　　　　　　　　　　　　　　　　　　　　　　a

訳　男性: かなり良い取引だと思うな。もし2ヵ月早く引き渡せたら、8％のボーナスがもらえるんだ。
　　女性: そうよ。でも、忘れないで、もし最終期限までに間に合わないと遅滞料を払わなければなりませんよ。
　　男性: では、すぐに電話して、彼らにこちらが受諾するということを知らせるべきだね。

Q　彼らは何をするのでしょうか。

　a. 電話をかける。　　　　　　b. 提案について論じる。
　c. 彼らの出荷について話す。　　d. 遅滞料を払う。

参考　男性の最後のコメントから取引がまだ受諾されてない事がわかる。

20.　基礎知識問題　　　　　　　　　　　　　　　　　　　b

訳　女性: あなたは全ての願書をもう読み終わりましたか。
　　男性: はい。しかし決定するのは難しいです。全員が素晴らしい資格を持っているようです。
　　女性: さてと、この職は月末までに満たされなければなりませんから、できるだけ早く決定しなければなりません。

Q　彼らは何について話しているのですか。

　a. 女性の資格。　　　　　　　b. 新入社員を雇う。
　c. 最高の地位を決める。　　　d. 月末に何をするか

参考　benefit「給付金」 allowance「手当て」 pension「年金」 wage「賃金」

21.　　　　　　　　　　　　　　　　　　　　　　　　　c

訳　女性: これらのサンプルを送るのに最も能率的な方法は何だと思う？
　　男性: パッケージ配達会社が一番速いです、但し、それよりは1週ほど長くかかりますが普通郵便が一番安いです。
　　女性: 配達会社で送りましょう。重要なのはお客様がそれらをできるだけ速く受け取れることです。

Q　彼らは何について話しているのですか。

　a. 彼らの製品を荷造りする必要性。　b. 最も安い方法。
　c. 製品サンプルを送る方法。　　　　d. 配達会社を見つけること。

参考　express mail「速達」 registered mail「書留」 money order「為替」

22.

Man: I'm worried about the inventory at the Chicago store. I think it's becoming too large.

Woman: I agree, but the holiday season is coming up soon, so most of it should be sold when it's over.

Man: I hope you're right. If not, we'll have to discount everything.

Q What are they discussing?

    a. The amount of inventory.   b. The size of the Chicago store.

    c. The coming holiday season. d. A discount sale.

23.

Man: Good evening, Ma'am. How can I help you?

Woman: I'd like a single room for one night. I'll pay by credit card, and my luggage is over by the door.

Man: Certainly. You'll be in 604. I'll have your bags sent up immediately.

Q What is the man's job?

    a. A bellman.   b. A porter.

    c. A doorman.   d. A front desk clerk.

24

Woman: Lewis, have you seen the market report? Ampex Incorporated is really taking off!

Man: Yes. I've been monitoring it quite closely. In fact, I just bought 1000 shares yesterday.

Woman: You did? Maybe I should pick some up too before the price gets too high.

Q What are they discussing?

    a. Going to the market.   b. How many shares Lewis bought.

    c. Purchasing stock.   d. A company's financial policy.

22.   a

訳 男性: 私はシカゴ店の在庫について心配しています。それが多くなりすぎていると思うのです。
女性: 同感です。しかし，休暇シーズンはすぐですし，そのほとんどがシーズン後に販売されるべきです。
男性: あなたが正しいと願っていますよ。もしそうでないとしたら全てを割引しなければならなくなります。

Q 彼らは何を議論しているのですか。
a. 在庫の量。   b. シカゴ店のサイズ。
c. 次の休暇シーズン。   d. 割引セール。

参考 inventory「在庫」 inventory day「棚卸の日」

23. 基礎知識問題   d

訳 男性: こんばんわ，奥様。いらっしゃいませ。
女性: シングル・ルームを一晩お願いします。支払いはクレジットカードでです。それと私の荷物はドアのそばにあります。
男性: 承知いたしました。604号です。お客様のバッグは直ちに部屋に運ばせます。

Q 男の仕事は何ですか。
a. ベルマン。   b. ポーター。
c. ドアマン。   d. フロント・デスク従業員。

参考 ホテルのチェックインの会話は要暗記。

24.   c

訳 女性: ルイス，市場レポートを見ましたか。アムペックス株式会社が本当によく売れていますよ。
男性: はい。ずっと注意してモニターしてきたのです。事実，私は昨日ちょうど1000株を買ったところです。
女性: そうですか。もしかしたら価格が高くなり過ぎる前に，私も何株か買うべきでしょう。

Q 彼らは何を話し合っているのですか。
a. 市場に行くこと。   b. ルイスが何株購入したか。
c. 株の購入。   d. 会社の財務方針。

参考 take off 物事がうまくいく，商品が急に売れ出す，景気が良くなる。

Part III 会話問題

25.

Man: How was your vacation? I hear New Zealand is beautiful at this time of year.
Woman: It certainly is, but all the facilities at our hotel had additional charges, so it turned out to be rather expensive.
Man: That's too bad. That's why before booking I always check to see what's included and what's not.

Q What are they talking about?
    a. Checking the books.   b. Extra hotel charges.
    c. Winter in New Zealand.   d. Additional vacation time.

26.

Woman: Our research department is going to expand. Have you heard about it yet?
Man: Yes, I have, and I've also heard they're buying 30 new computers.
Woman: At this rate, we'll have one of the best in the country.

Q What is this discussion about?
    a. The quality of the research.
    b. Expenditure cuts.
    c. The growth rate of the company.
    d. Buying new computers.

27.

Man: The consultants suggest that if we want to attract the best personnel, we should improve our incentive package.
Woman: Really? I thought offering higher salaries would get us the most qualified people.
Man: They're the experts, so I think we ought to follow their advice.

Q What are the man and woman talking about?
    a. Hiring new employees.   b. Improving the packaging system.
    c. The high cost of salaries.   d. Their expertise.

解答
b

25.

訳 男性: あなたの休暇はどうでしたか。この時期のニュージーランドは美しいと聞いています。
女性: 確かにそうですが、ホテルの全設備が割増し料金になっていて思っていたより高くつきました。
男性: それは残念でしたね。そのようなことがあるので私は予約する前にいつも何が含まれ、何が含まれてないかをチェックするのです。

Q 彼らは何について話しているのですか。
　a. 本をチェックしている。　　　b. 割増ホテル料金。
　c. 冬のニュージーランド。　　　d. 追加の休暇時間。

参考 occupancy rate「稼働率」　valet service「クリーニングサービス」

26.

解答
d

訳 女性: 当社の研究部は拡張します。もうそれについてはもう聞きました？
男性: はい。新しいコンピュータを30台買っているとも聞いています。
女性: この分では国中で最高の研究部の1つを持つことになりますね。

Q このディスカッションは何についてですか。
　a. 彼らの研究の質。　　　　b. 経費削減。
　c. 会社の成長率。　　　　　d. 新しいコンピュータを買うこと。

参考 expenditure「経費」　overhead「諸経費」
　　 expense account「接待費」

27.

解答
a

訳 男性: コンサルタントが提案している事は、もし我々が最高の人員を引きつけたいならば、奨励金制度を改善しなければならないということです。
女性: そうですね。高い給料を提供すれば最適任者を獲得できると思いましたのに。
男性: 彼らは専門家ですから、彼らの忠告に従うべきだと思います。

Q 男性と女性は何について話しているのですか。
　a. 新しい従業員を雇うこと。　　b. 包装システムを改善すること。
　c. 給料のコストが高いこと。　　d. 彼らの専門知識。

参考 incentive「報奨, 奨励金」　expertise「専門知識」

Part III 会話問題

28.

Woman: My husband and I are looking for a place with a large yard, three bedrooms, in an area with good schools.
Man: I think I have just what you're looking for. It's over on Pine Street. Would you like to see it?
Woman: Yes. Would sometime tomorrow be convenient?

Q What is the man's job?

    a. A part-time worker.
    b. A schoolteacher.
    c. A convenience store manager.
    d. A real estate agent.

29.

Man: Do we have a list of clients who placed orders within the last three years?
Woman: No, there's no one list that covers all three years, but we do have lists for each individual year.
Man: Thanks. I think I'll have my assistant get them and compile them into a master list.

Q What is this conversation about?

    a. Their wrists.
    b. Client complaints.
    c. Company records.
    d. His assistant's job.

30.

Woman: I just found out that Tyco is planning to build a new store three blocks from here.
Man: I can't believe it. Do you think it will affect our sales?
Woman: I think it'll depend on the size of the building and the type of merchandise they'll carry.

Q What are they discussing?

    a. Keeping merchandise.
    b. The plans for a new building.
    c. The effect of sales.
    d. Their competition.

28.   d

訳 女性: 私の夫と私は，良い学校がある地域で，大きい庭とベッドルーム3部屋があるところを探しています。
男性: あなたがちょうどお捜しのものがあります。それはパイン・ストリートにありますが，ご覧になりたいですか。
女性: はい，明日のいつ頃が都合が良いですか。

Q 男性の仕事は何ですか。
a. パートタイマー。　　　　　b. 学校教師。
c. コンビニのマネージャー。　d. 不動産仲介人。

29.   c

訳 男性: この3年以内で注文を出したクライアントのリストがありますか。
女性: いいえ，3年全部をカバーするリストはありませんが，年度ごとのリストはあります。
男性: 有難う。私のアシスタントにそれらを集めて編集してもらいマスター・リストすることにします。

Q この会話は何についてですか。
a. 彼らの手首。　　　　b. 依頼人の苦情。
c. 会社の記録。　　　　d. 彼のアシスタントの仕事。

参考 compile 編纂する，編集する

30.   d

訳 女性: タイコ社がここから3ブロック離れたところに新しい店舗を建てることになっていると知ったところです。
男性: 信じられません。当社の販売に影響を及ぼすと思いますか。
女性: 建物のサイズと彼らが置く商品のタイプによると思います。

Q 彼らは何を話し合っているのですか。
a. 商品を保存すること。　b. 新しい建物の計画。
c. セールスの効果。　　　d. 彼らの競争。

参考 男性のコメント中の affect our sales と女性の最後のコメントで d だとわかる。

Part III 会話問題

31.

Man: I don't care about the cost. I want that shipment sent out by four o'clock today.
Woman: In that case, I'll call an express trucking company. They'll have it to you by three.
Man: It better be, or else I'll run out of cloth.

Q Who is the man?

   a. A tailor.
   b. A shipper.
   c. A trucker.
   d. A laundry man.

32.

Man: That was the dirtiest taxi I've ever been in.
Woman: I know. It's even worse than that one last summer in Paris.
Man: Why doesn't the company clean them before they go out each day?

Q What's wrong with the taxi?

   a. It's not clean.
   b. It doesn't have an air-conditioner.
   c. It's dangerous.
   d. It smells bad.

33.

Woman: The company can't really afford it now, but we have no choice. These printing presses are just too old.
Man: Prices are really high now. Can we wait another six or eight months?
Woman: If we want to stay competitive, we'll have to get new ones right away.

Q What is this conversation about?

   a. Publishing books.
   b. Printing a photo.
   c. The high cost of printing.
   d. Replacing their machinery.

解答

31.　　　　　　　　　　　　　　　　　　　　　　　a

訳　男性: コストはどうでもいいですから，今日の4時までに例の荷を出荷したいのです。
　　女性: そういう場合でしたら，トラック運送会社に電話をかけましょう。あなたのところに3時までに届けてもらいます。
　　男性: そうした方がいい。さもなければ布地が尽きてしまう。

Q　男性の職業は何ですか。

　a. 洋服屋。　　　　　　　　　b. 船荷主。
　c. トラック運転手。　　　　　d. 洗濯屋。

参考　I'll run out of cloth で解答が明確になります。

32.　基礎知識問題　　　　　　　　　　　　　　　　a

訳　男性: あれは私がこれまでに乗ったタクシーで一番汚かったぞ。
　　女性: 本当ね。去年の夏にパリで乗ったのよりひどいわ。
　　男性: 会社は彼らが出庫する前にどうして毎日掃除しないのだろう？

Q　タクシーの何がいけないのですか。

　a. 清潔でない。　　　　　　　b. 空調が無い。
　c. 危険だ。　　　　　　　　　d. 臭う。

参考　男性の冒頭コメントと女性の言葉まで聞くと解答が特定できる。
　　　that one (which we took) last summer in Paris.

33.　　　　　　　　　　　　　　　　　　　　　　　d

訳　女性: 会社は現在本当に余裕はありませんが，我々には選択の余地がありません。これらの印刷機は古すぎます。
　　男性: 現在，価格は非常に高いですよ。もう6ヵ月か8ヵ月待てますか。
　　女性: もし当社が競争力を保持していたいのなら，今，新しいものを入手しなければなりません。

Q　この会話は何についてですか。

　a. 本の出版。　　　　　　　　b. 写真を焼きつける。
　c. 印刷コストが高い。　　　　d. 彼らの機械を交換すること。

参考　competitive「（品質，性能，価格が）他に負けない，競争力がある」

34.

Woman: Hello Steve. We're going to have a planning meeting here at the main building this afternoon. Are you coming?

Man: Hi Terry. I'm sorry, but I can't make it. But I'm sending my assistant, Ms. Sanchez, in my place.

Woman: In that case, make sure she brings the summary for the United Oil account.

Q What is Steve's problem?

    a. He canceled the meeting. b. He can't attend the meeting.
    c. He has to assist his boss. d. He couldn't make the summary.

35.

Man: This seems like the slowest train I've ever been on.

Woman: I know. That's because we're in the middle of rush hour and also because of the heavy rain.

Man: It's really bad timing. I just hope we can make our appointment with Mrs. Eastman by three.

Q What is their main concern?

    a. The training schedule. b. Finding a faster train.
    c. Keeping their appointment. d. The weather forecast.

36.

Woman: I'm sorry your order of engine parts was delayed.

Man: What was the reason, Ms. Galvan? Did your shipping department make a mistake?

Woman: No, it went out on time, but there was an accident on the highway from the factory.

Q What was the man's problem?

    a. There was an accident on the ship.
    b. His components were lost.
    c. There was an accident at the firm.
    d. His shipment didn't arrive on time.

解答
b

34.

訳 女性: こんにちは，スティーブ，本館で今日の午後に企画会議がありますが，あなたはいらっしゃるのですか。
男性: やあ，テリー，すみませんがだめなのです。でも，私の助手のサンチェスさんを代りに出しますよ。
女性: その場合，彼女がユナイテッド・オイル社の概要を絶対に持って来てくださるようにしてください。

Q スティーブの問題は何ですか。
  a. 彼はミーティングを中止した。
  b. 彼はミーティングに出席できない。
  c. 彼は彼の上司を手伝わなければならない。
  d. 彼は概要を作ることができなかった。

35. c

訳 男性: これは今までに乗った電車の中で一番遅いように思える。
女性: そうね。ラッシュアワーの最中で，その上，大雨が降っていることでもあるしね。
男性: 本当にタイミングが悪いね。イーストマン夫人と3時までに会う約束を守れることを願っているよ。

Q 彼らが主に心配していることは何ですか。
  a. トレーニングのスケジュール。   b. より速い電車を見つけること。
  c. 彼らの約束を守ること。   d. 天気予報。

参考 concern「懸念，心配，関心事，利害関係，会社」

36. d

訳 女性: すみません，あなたのエンジン・パーツのご注文が遅れました。
男性: どんな理由でですか，ガルバンさん？ 発送部が間違ったのですか。
女性: いいえ，時間通りに出荷したのですが，工場からの道すがらハイウェイで事故があったのです。

Q 男性は何で困ったのですか。
  a. 船で事故があった。   b. 彼の部品がなくなった。
  c. 会社で事故があった。   d. 彼の荷物が時間通りに到着しなかった。

参考 女性の言葉からdelayが問題になっていることが明確になっている。

37.

Man: Where's the personnel manager? I have to see him right away.
Woman: He's not in at the moment. Is there anything I can do for you?
Man: Yes, I've heard rumors that my entire section will be laid off and I want to find out if they're true.

Q Why is the man upset?

    a. He's afraid of losing his job.   b. His section is taking the day off.
    c. He made a mistake in calculation. d. The manager was fired.

38.

Woman: We placed an order over a month ago for 5,000 envelopes and we still haven't received it.
Man: I'm aware of that, but there was a fire at our plant two weeks ago and production is behind. We'll get your order out ASAP.
Woman: I hope you do. Our mailing department can only operate for three more days with our current stock.

Q What is the woman's problem?

    a. The price of her stock is going down.
    b. Her order is late.
    c. There was an explosion in the factory.
    d. There wasn't any stationery.

39.

Man: The sub-contractor has a week to finish the wiring before the walls can be put up.
Woman: I hope he can make the deadline. The whole project will be behind schedule if he doesn't.
Man: I know. That's why I've called in extra electricians to work with him. They're experts and can work really fast.

Q What did the man do?

    a. He got extra electricians.
    b. He rescheduled their project.
    c. He dismissed the sub-contractor.
    d. He had the walls demolished.

37. a

訳 男性: 人事部長はどこですか。 すぐに彼に会わなければなりません。
女性: ただ今，席を外しております。何か私にできることはありますか。
男性: はい。私の課全員が解雇されるといううわさを聞きましたので，それが本当かどうか知りたいのです。

Q 男性はなぜ動揺しているのですか。
 a. 彼は仕事を失う事を恐れている。 b. 彼の課はその日休暇をとっている。
 c. 彼は誤算した。 d. 部長が解雇された。

参考 personnel department = human resources department「人事部」

38. b

訳 女性: 1ヵ月以上前に封筒5,000枚の注文を出したのですが，まだそれを受け取っておりません。
男性: 承知はしているのですが，2週間前に当社の工場で火事があり生産が遅れているのです。御社の注文品を至急発送いたします。
女性: お願いしますよ。当社の郵送部は現在の在庫では3日間しか操業できません。

Q 女性の問題は何ですか。
 a. 彼女の在庫品の価格が下がっている。
 b. 彼女の注文品が遅れている。
 c. 工場で爆発があった。 d. 便箋が全く無かった。

参考 be aware of「～に気づいている」　ASAP = as soon as possible

39. a

訳 男性: 壁を張る前に，下請け業者が配線を終えるのに1週間かかります。
女性: 最終期限までできるといいのですが，さもないと，全プロジェクトが予定より遅れることになります。
男性: そうです。それで電気技術者を臨時に増員したのです。彼らは専門家ですから迅速に仕事してくれますよ。

Q 男性は何をしたのですか。
 a. 電気技術者を増員した。 b. プロジェクトの日程を変更した。
 c. 下請け業者を解任した。 d. 壁を解体させた。

参考 make the deadline「期限に間に合う」
have+物+過去分詞　「物を～させる」　demolish「破壊する」

40.

Woman: There are a couple of boxes missing from this shipment of company documents.
Man: I'll call the trucking company and check their shipping invoice.
Woman: Please do, and notify me as soon as you have some information. They all have to be mailed by Friday.

Q What does the man need to do?

    a. Phone the trucking company.   b. Notify the truckers.
    c. Mail the invoice.   d. Check the boxes.

41.

Man: I have to take a company car to a sales meeting today, but I can't find the sign-out sheet. Have you seen it?
Woman: The last time I saw it, Mr. McGraw had it.
Man: We should make it a policy to keep that sheet in one place so it's easy to find.

Q What is the man's problem?

    a. He's late for a meeting.   b. He can't sign out a car.
    c. It's in her drawer.   d. They have to make a policy.

42.

Woman: This table is too close to the kitchen. It's too loud.
Man: I know. I'll call the waiter and see if we can change tables.
Woman: Good. Try to get one by the window in the non-smoking area.

Q What is their problem?

    a. There's too much smoke.   b. The tables are too close.
    c. It's too noisy.   d. They can't change tables.

40.   a

訳 女性: 会社の書類が入った箱が2つ，この荷の中にありません。
   男性: トラック運送会社に電話して，彼らの輸送送り状をチェックしましょう。
   女性: そうしてください。なにか情報がわかったらすぐに知らせてください。全書類を金曜日までに送付しなければなりません。

Q 男性は何をする必要があるのですか。
   a. トラック運送会社に電話する。　b. トラック運転手に通知する。
   c. 送り状を郵送する。　　　　　　d. 箱を調べる。

・・・・・・・・・・・・・・・・・・・・・・・・・・・・・

参考 男性は電話し，女性は送り状を郵送する。

41.   b

訳 男性: 私は，今日，社の車で販売会議へ行かなければならないのですが，使用証明書が見つかりません。見ましたか。
   女性: 私が最後にそれを見たときは，マックグロー氏が持っていました。
   男性: 簡単に見つけられるように，シートを一ヶ所に置く決まりにするべきです。

Q 男性の問題は何ですか。
   a. 彼は会議に遅れる。　　　　　　b. 車を使うための署名ができない。
   c. それは彼女の引出しの中にある。d. 方針を立てなければならない。

・・・・・・・・・・・・・・・・・・・・・・・・・・・・・

参考 使用証明書が見つからない。＝ 車が使えない。

42.   c

訳 女性: このテーブルは台所に近すぎるわ。音がうるさすぎるわ。
   男性: そうだね。ウェイターを呼んでテーブルを変えられるか見てみよう。
   女性: それが良いわ。禁煙席の窓の側にできるか試しに聞いてみて。

Q 彼らの問題は何ですか。
   a. 煙が多すぎる。　　　　　　　　b. テーブル同士が近すぎる。
   c. 雑音が多すぎる。　　　　　　　d. テーブルを変えることができない。

・・・・・・・・・・・・・・・・・・・・・・・・・・・・・

参考 冒頭の女性のコメントで解答が判断できる。

Part III 会話問題

43.

Man: I requested an aisle seat when I made the reservation.
Woman: I'm sorry, sir, but the flight is fully booked. All we can give you is a center seat.
Man: I guess I have no choice, but I don't like it. Center seats are a tight squeeze.

Q What is his complaint?

    a. He requested a reservation.
    b. The flight is fully booked.
    c. He squeezed too tightly.
    d. He didn't get the seat he wanted.

44.

Man: Ms. Whitney, I'd like to hear what you have to say about the timing of the merger with Eastern Electronics.
Woman: Well, I think the scheduled date in November is OK, but I believe that it would be in our interest to do it in February after the dividends are announced.
Man: That's a very valid point. I'll take it under consideration.

Q What is the man's opinion of Ms. Whitney's point?

    a. It's a good idea.   b. Her timing is way off.
    c. November is OK.   d. She's very considerate.

45.

Man: Have you gone over those contracts I put on your desk this morning?
Woman: No, sorry, I haven't. I was in court all morning with a client.
Man: I understand, but could you get to it as soon as you can? They have to be mailed by Thursday.

Q What is the woman's profession?

    a. A sub-contractor.   b. A tennis teacher.
    c. A lawyer.   d. An executive.

43. 基礎知識問題

解答 **d**

訳 男性: 予約した時に通路席をお願いしました。
女性: 申し訳ないのですが，当便は満席なのです。さしあげられるのが中央の座席だけなのです。
男性: 選ぶ余地はなさそうですね。でも嫌になりますね。中央の座席は窮屈ですから。

Q 彼の不満は何ですか。
 a. 彼は予約を要請した。　　b. フライトは満席だ。
 c. 彼はきつく握りすぎた。　d. 彼は自分が欲しかった席をとれなかった。

参考 squeeze「強く握る，絞る」

44.

解答 **a**

訳 男性: ホイットニーさん，Eastern Electronicsとの合併のタイミングについてのあなたの意見を聞かせていただきたいです。
女性: ええと，私は11月の予定日は良いと思いますが，私は配当が発表された後，2月にそれをするのが当社には有利であると思います。
男性: 非常にごもっともです。それを考慮に入れましょう。

Q ホイットニーさんの観点に対して男性の意見はどうですか。
 a. 良い考えである。　　　b. タイミングが全くずれている。
 c. 11月が良い。　　　　　d. 彼女は非常に思慮深いです。

参考 merger「合併」　dividend「配当」

45.

解答 **c**

訳 男性: 今朝あなたの机の上に私が置いておいた契約書を検討しましたか。
女性: いいえ，ごめんなさい。クライアントといっしょに午前中はずっと法廷にいたのです。
男性: わかりました，でもできるだけ速くそれに取りかかって下さい。それらを木曜日までに郵送しなければならないのです。

Q 女性の職業は何ですか。
 a. 下請け。　　　　　　　b. テニスの先生。
 c. 弁護士。　　　　　　　d. 重役。

参考 in court「法廷で」　court「裁判所，宮廷，コート，中庭」

46.

Woman: Peter, there's a Mr. Murry here to see you. He doesn't have an appointment.
Man: Oh, he's from the advertising agency. Tell him I'll be with him in about 10 minutes.
Woman: OK, I'll let him know.

Q What is the woman's position?

a. A receptionist.
b. A reservationist.
c. An advertising agent.
d. An answering service employee.

47.

Woman: These figures for the Sternman audit can't be right. They're much too high.
Man: I checked them three times and I couldn't find anything wrong.
Woman: Did you remember to subtract the cost of equipment depreciation?

Q What are their jobs?

a. Equipment suppliers.
b. Accountants.
c. Machine inspectors.
d. Salespeople.

48.

Man: This computer comes in three models and is easily upgradable.
Woman: Well, I'm mostly interested in running large graphics programs. Which model would you suggest?
Man: I would suggest the CRX-45. It's our top of the line.

Q What is the man's occupation?

a. A computer programmer.
b. A desk clerk.
c. A salesman.
d. A graphic designer.

46. 基礎知識問題 a

訳 女性: ピーター，こちらにマリー氏という方がいらっしゃってあなたにお会いになりたいとのことです。予約はないそうです。
男性: ああ，彼は広告代理店の人です。10分したらお会いすると伝えて下さい。
女性: はい。彼にお伝えします。

Q 女性の職は何ですか。

a. 受付係 b. 予約受付係
c. 広告代理業者 d. 伝言サービスの従業員

参考 受付係の表現問題は400点台到達を目指す人には落せないもの。

47. b

訳 女性: スターマン監査の数字は正しいはずがないわ。高すぎるわ。
男性: 私は3回チェックしましたが，何もおかしいところを見つけられませんでした。
女性: 設備減価償却費を差し引くのを覚えていましたか。

Q 彼らの仕事は何ですか。

a. 備品供給元 b. 会計係
c. 機械検査官 d. 販売員

参考 audit「監査する」 depreciation「減価償却，価格低下」

48. c

訳 男性: このコンピュータには3つの型があり簡単にアップグレードができます。
女性: ええと，私の興味があるのは主に，大きいグラフィック・プログラムを実行することです。どのモデルがお勧めですか。
男性: CRX-45をお勧めします。当社の最高級品です。

Q 男の仕事は何ですか。

a. コンピュータ・プログラマー b. 事務員
c. セールスマン d. グラフィック・デザイナー

参考 top of the line「トップ商品，最高級品」

Part III 会話問題

49.

Woman: Were you able to look over the budget figures for the annual report?
Man: Yes, I did, and everything seems fine, but I did want to talk about the high proportion of transportation costs.
Woman: I did as well. Why don't we go over them some time before the end of the week?

Q What is this conversation about?
    a. A meeting at the end of the week.
    b. Excessive shipping costs.
    c. The next annual report.
    d. How to transport merchandise.

50.

Man: Are you going to speak about the new quota system at the meeting today?
Woman: Yes, I'm not happy with the current sales volume. I think the staff can do much better. Anyone who doesn't meet their new quota will be let go.
Man: Some of the staff might not be too happy with that idea.

Q What is the woman's job?
    a. A technician.   b. A manager.
    c. A chauffeur.   d. A public speaker.

51.

Woman: In my opinion these bonds mature much too late for a short-term investment.
Man: Then, what else would you recommend?
Woman: You should put your money in either technology or oil stocks. These look better for the short-term.

Q What does the woman think about the bonds?
    a. Technology and oil stocks are less risky.
    b. They're fine for the short-term.
    c. They're not good for short-term investment.
    d. It's too late to buy them.

49.　　　　　　　　　　　　　　　　　　　　　　　b

訳　女性: 年次報告の予算の数字に目を通せましたか。
　　男性: はい。全てが良いようですが，輸送コストの割合の高さについてはお話をしたいと思っていました。
　　女性: 私もです。週末前のいつかにそれらを詳しく調べませんか。

Q この会話は何についてですか。
　a. 週末のミーティング。　　　b. 過度の輸送コスト。
　c. 次期年次報告。　　　　　　d. 商品を輸送する方法。

参考　annual「年1度の，年次」　proportion「割合」
　　　excessive「過度の」

50.　　　　　　　　　　　　　　　　　　　　　　　b

訳　男性: あなたは今日の会議で新しい割当制度について話されますか。
　　女性: はい，私は現在の販売量に満足していないのです。スタッフはもっとできると思います。新しい割当数を出せない人は首になります。
　　男性: スタッフの中にはその考えをあまり歓迎しない人たちもいるかもしれませんよ。

Q 女性の仕事は何ですか。
　a. テクニシャン。　　　　　　b. マネージャー。
　c. お抱え運転手。　　　　　　d. 演説者。

参考　この女性は従業員を解雇できる地位にある。quota「割当」

51.　　　　　　　　　　　　　　　　　　　　　　　c

訳　女性: 短期投資としては，これらの債券が満期になるのが遅すぎるのではないかと思います。
　　男性: では，あなたは他に何を推薦します？
　　女性: テクノロジーまたは石油の株式に投資するべきだと思います。短期向けにはこれらの方がよいでしょう。

Q 債券について女性はどのようなことを考えていますか。
　a. テクノロジーと石油の株式が危険が少ない。
　b. それらは短期用として素晴らしい。
　c. それらは短期の投資に向いていない。
　d. それらを買うには遅すぎる。

52.

Man: I'd rather not take the train to the meeting in Boston, even though it's only two hours away.
Woman: I know. It's very slow and inconvenient.
Man: That's why I feel that generally, people like to fly there from here.

Q What does the man think?
  a. The train is economical.   b. Most people prefer to fly.
  c. It's generally inconvenient. d. Many people don't fly.

53.

Man: According to all the newspapers and magazines, all the indicators point to a slide in the market.
Woman: How accurate do you think they are?
Man: Considering the number of experts in agreement, I would have to go along with them, too.

Q What does the man think will happen?
  a. He will go along with the market.
  b. The experts will write magazines.
  c. He will think about the contract.
  d. Stock prices will go down.

54.

Woman: The number of copies being made recently has really gone up. This is costing us a great deal in paper, not to mention copy machine repairs.
Man: What can we do to solve this problem?
Woman: I think we should limit the number of copies that each employee can make in a month.

Q What is the woman's opinion?
  a. Cut the number of copies. b. Limit the number of employees.
  c. Repair the copy machine.   d. Think about it for a month.

52.   b

訳 男性: ボストンの会議場までは2時間の距離ですが，私は電車で行きたくはありません。
女性: そうですね。非常に遅いし，不便ですから。
男性: そういうことで，通常，皆がここからそこまで飛行機で行くのだと思います。

Q 男性は何を考えているのですか。
 a. 電車は安い。　　　　　　b. ほとんどの人々は飛行機で行く方を好む。
 c. 一般的に不便です。　　　d. 多くの人々は飛行機で行かない。

参考 C は何が不便なのか特定できないし，「不便だ」と言っているのは女性。

53.   d

訳 男性: あらゆる新聞と雑誌によると，(経済)指標のほとんどが市場での下落の傾向を示しています。
女性: それらはどのくらい正確だと思います？
男性: 同意見の専門家の数を考慮すると，私も彼らに同意しなければならないでしょう。

Q 男性は何が起こると思っていますか。
 a. 彼は市場に同調する。　　　b. 全専門家は雑誌を書く。
 c. 彼は契約について考える。　d. 株価が下がる。

参考 indicator「指標」　point to「傾向を示す，暗示する」
slide「下落」

54.   a

訳 女性: 最近コピーの量が非常に多くなってきています。コピー機修理は言うまでもなく，紙代も相当なものです。
男性: この問題を解決するために何かできるでしょうか。
女性: 従業員ひとりあたりが1ヵ月間にコピーできる枚数を制限するべきだと思います。

Q 女性の意見は何ですか。
 a. コピーの枚数を削減する。　b. 従業員数を制限する
 c. コピー機を修理する。　　　d. それについて1ヵ月考える。

55.

Woman: Kurt, what's the matter, you don't look too happy?
Man: I just came out of a meeting with the board of directors. They really criticized the report I'd been working on for a month for lacking enough facts.
Woman: That's too bad, but now you know what to do for your next report.

Q What did the board think of the report?
    a. It didn't have enough facts.   b. It wasn't long enough.
    c. He worked for a month.   d. They liked it well enough.

56.

Man: Do we have any idea what our lawyers are charging us on a yearly basis?
Woman: I'm not exactly sure, but I know it's quite high.
Man: I think it's about time the company considered forming its own legal department.

Q In the man's opinion, what should the company do?
    a. Get a new law firm.   b. Employ staff lawyers.
    c. Charge on a yearly basis.   d. Think about the time.

57.

Woman: Hey, Hiroshi, why don't we take Professor Riseman's business management class this Spring?
Man: I heard his lectures are really boring and he gives a lot of homework.
Woman: That may be true, but he's one of the leading experts in the field, and I feel we could learn a lot from him.

Q What is the woman's opinion of Prof. Riseman?
    a. He's not truthful.
    b. He is a knowledgeable teacher.
    c. He exerts himself in the field.
    d. He gives too much homework.

解答

55.　　　　　　　　　　　　　　　　　　　　　　　　　　a

訳　女性: カート，どうしたのですか，あまりハッピーではなさそうですね。
　　男性: 私は取締役会と会合してきたところです。私が1ヵ月取り組んできたレポートに対して十分な事実が無いと非常に批判されました。
　　女性: それは残念ですね，でも，これであなたの次のレポートをどうするべきかわかったでしょう。

Q　取締役会はレポートをどう考えましたか。
　a. 十分な事実記述がなかった。　　b. 十分な長さがなかった。
　c. 彼は1ヵ月働いた。　　　　　　d. 彼等はそれをかなり気に入った。

参考　男性のコメントがカギです。　criticize「批判する」

56.　　　　　　　　　　　　　　　　　　　　　　　　　　b

訳　男性: 私たちの弁護士の請求する年間料金がどのくらいか知っていますか？
　　女性: 正確には知りませんが，かなり高いことは知っています。
　　男性: 私は会社自体で法律部門を組織することを考えてもいい時期に来ていると思います。

Q　男性の意見によると会社は何をするべきですか。
　a. 新しい法律事務所と契約する。　b. 社員弁護士を雇う。
　c. 年間方式で請求する。　　　　　d. 時間のことを考える。

参考　legal advisor「法律顧問」　legitimate business「合法的な商売」

57.　　　　　　　　　　　　　　　　　　　　　　　　　　b

訳　女性: 弘さん，この春期はライズマン教授のビジネス管理クラスを取りませんか。
　　男性: 彼の講義は本当に退屈だそうですよ，しかも宿題もたくさん出すそうです。
　　女性: それはそうかもしれませんが，彼はその分野で一流の専門家の1人ですし，彼から多くの事を学べるのではないかと思います。

Q　ライズマン教授に関する女性の意見はどのようなものですか。
　a. 彼は正直ではない。　　　　　　b. 彼は見識のある先生である。
　c. 彼は現場で奮闘する。　　　　　d. 彼は宿題をたくさん与え過ぎる。

参考　knowledgeable「見識のある，精通している」　ついでにerudite「学識がある」という単語も覚えよう。

58.

Man: It's my belief that the specifications for the new hard drives are perfect for our current mid-size frames.

Woman: I agree. The company will save a great deal by using the frames already in stock.

Man: Then it's settled. Let's move on to the next item on the agenda.

Q What does the woman think?

    a. The mid-size frames are too small.

    b. They should buy the stocks now.

    c. The hard drives will be cost effective.

    d. She doubts the specifications.

59.

Woman: Frankly Allan, for all the overtime and weekend work I do for this company, I don't feel I get adequate compensation.

Man: If I were you, I'd keep track of all the extra hours you put in, write it up, present it to the department manager, then, ask for a raise.

Woman: That's a good idea. I might just do that.

Q What does Allan think she should do?

    a. Write to the trucker.   b. Give the manager a present.

    c. Stop working extra hours.   d. Say she wants a higher wage.

60.

Man: When is the concrete company scheduled to deliver the first load?

Woman: I'm not sure exactly, but I think it's due sometime on Wednesday afternoon.

Man: That's no good. We need it in the morning because my plans call for the frame to be erected in the afternoon.

Q What is the man's occupation?

    a. A deliveryman.   b. An architect.

    c. A sales representative.   d. A shipping clerk.

	解答

58.   c

訳 男性: 新しいハード・ドライブの仕様は現在の中型のフレームにちょうど良いと思います。
女性: 同感です。会社はすでに手持ちのフレームを使用して相当の節約ができます。
男性: では，決まった。次の議事事項に進みましょう。

Q 女性の考えはどうですか。
a. 中型フレームはあまりに小さすぎる。　b. 彼らは株を購入するべきである。
c. ハード・ドライブは費用有効度が高いでしょう。
d. 彼女は仕様書がおかしいと思っている。

参考 specification「仕様，明細」　agenda「議事事項」は必須単語。

59.   d

訳 女性: 率直に言うと，アラン，会社のために私が費やしている全ての時間外と週末の仕事にたいして適切な報酬を受けていないと感じるのです。
男性: もし私があなただったら，時間外の記録をとっておいて文書にして，それを部長に提出し，昇給してくれるように頼みます。
女性: それは良い考えですね。そうしてみようかしら。

Q アランは彼女が何をするべきだと思っていますか。
a. トラック運送業者に手紙を書く。b. 部長にプレゼントする。
c. 時間外の仕事を止める。　　　　d. より高額の賃金が欲しいと言う。

参考 compensation「報酬，棒給，補償」

60.   b

訳 男性: コンクリート会社はいつ最初の荷を配達する事になっていますか。
女性: はっきりとはわかりませんが，水曜日の午後のいつかが納入期限だと思います。
男性: それではだめです。午前中にそれが必要なのです。私の計画では午後にはフレームを立てなければなりません。

Q 男性の仕事は何ですか。
a. 配達人　　　　　　　　　　b. 建築家
c. 営業マン　　　　　　　　　d. 発送係

参考 erect「組み立てる，建築する」　建築資材を要求できるのは誰か。

61.

Woman: Excuse me, I'd like to speak with someone about opening a new account.

Man: I'm sorry Ma'am, but this is the commercial account section. You should go to the customer service section in the lobby on the first floor.

Woman: Thank you. I'll go there right now.

Q What does the man suggest?

    a. To go the customer service section.
    b. To open a commercial account.
    c. To go to the lobby first.
    d. To go to the service station.

62.

Woman: Hi Phil, what are your plans for the weekend?

Man: I'm going to be restoring my antique car. I've been working on it for weeks and want to have it ready for the antique car show next month in San Diego.

Woman: It's a nice car. Have you ever considered putting it up for sale after the show?

Q When will the antique car show be held?

    a. Over the weekend.   b. In four weeks.
    c. Next month.   d. In July.

63.

Man: Rina, where are you going in such a hurry?

Woman: I'm trying to make the bank by five. I'm running late and I have a big deposit to make.

Man: Next time you should make sure you give yourself enough time.

Q What is the man's advice?

    a. That she's running in a hurry.   b. That she leave earlier.
    c. To go next time.   d. To make sure of the time.

解答

61.　a

訳　女性：すみませんが，新しい口座を開設することについてどなたかとお話したいのですが。
　　男性：恐れ入りますが奥様，ここは商用口座のセクションです。一階ロビーにあるお客様相談窓口へお出で下さい。
　　女性：有難うございます。すぐそこに行きます。

Q 男性は何をするように勧めているのですか。
　a. 顧客相談窓口に行くこと。
　b. 商用口座を開設すること。
　c. 最初にロビーに行くこと。
　d. サービス・ステーションに行くこと。

参考　男性のコメントを聞いた時点で解答ができる。

62.　基礎知識問題　c

訳　女性：こんにちはフィル，あなたの週末の計画はどうなっていますか。
　　男性：私のアンティークカーを修復するつもりです。何週間も取り組んできたのです。それを来月サンディエゴで行われるアンティークカーショーに出す準備をしておきたいのです。
　　女性：素晴らしい車ですね。ショーの後にそれを売りに出してみることを考えたことはありますか。

Q アンティークカーのショーはいつ開かれるのですか。
　a. 週末にかけて。　　　b. 4週したら。
　c. 来月。　　　　　　　d. 7月に。

参考　restore「元の状態に戻す，回復する，修復する」

63.　b

訳　男性：リーナ，そんなに大急ぎでどこに行くのですか。
　　女性：5時までに銀行に行き着きたいのです。遅くなってしまいましたし，大金を預金しなければならないのです。
　　男性：次回は，十分に時間の余裕を取っておくようにするべきですね。

Q 男性のアドバイスは何ですか。
　a. 彼女が急ぐように。　　b. 彼女がもっと早く出るように。
　c. 次の時に行くこと。　　d. 時間を確かめること。

参考　give someone time「(人に) 猶予を与える」

Part III 会話問題　181

64.

Man: For a new office assistant I want to hire someone with some bookkeeping experience.
Woman: Yes, and I'd also like to have someone who's taken some business administration courses as well.
Man: In that case, I think we're going to have to go to a private employment agency to find someone with those qualifications.

Q What does the man suggest?
 a. Hire a skilled agent.
 b. Fire the new office assistant.
 c. Use an employment agency.
 d. Get some qualifications.

65.

Man: It's going to take at least five days to visit every customer on my sales route. The problem is, I have to go to the convention in three days.
Woman: Well, if you can't visit them all, why don't you just stop at the ones that you're sure will place an order?
Man: That's a good idea, but I'd rather concentrate on those that only "might" place an order.

Q What is the woman's advice to the man?
 a. To go to the convention in three days.
 b. To wait until he's sure.
 c. To visit the richest customers only.
 d. To stop at the best customers.

66.

Man: Can I cash a personal check here?
Woman: I'm sorry, sir, we only cash payroll or travelers checks. You might try the bank around the corner.
Man: OK, thanks a lot.

Q What is her advice?
 a. To cash a payroll check.
 b. To go to a bank.
 c. To check the cash.
 d. To wait on the corner.

64.　　　　　　　　　　　　　　　　　　　　　　　　c

訳　男性：新しいオフィス・アシスタントには，簿記経験が多少ある人を雇いたいと思います。
　　女性：そうですね。それに経営管理学を勉強した人が欲しいです。
　　男性：それでは，そのような資格を持った人を見つけるには私立職業紹介所へ行かなければならないと思います。

Q 男性は何を提案していますか。
　a. 熟練した代理人を雇う。　b. 新しいオフィス・アシスタントを解雇する。
　c. 職業紹介所を使う。　　　d. 資格を得る。

参考　business administration「経営管理」
　　　employment agency「職業安定所」

65.　　　　　　　　　　　　　　　　　　　　　　　　d

訳　男性：私の販売のルートで全顧客を訪問するには，少なくとも5日かかります。問題は，3日したら私は大会に行かなければならないのです。
　　女性：そうねえ，もしあなたが全員を訪問できないなら，注文を出してくれると確信が持てる人たちのところだけ立ち寄ったらどうですか。
　　男性：それは良い考えですね，でも私はむしろ"注文するかもしれない"人たちに集中したいと思います。

Q 女性から男性へのアドバイスは何ですか。
　a. 3日して大会に行くこと。
　b. 彼が確信するまで待つこと。
　c. 最も金持ちの顧客だけを訪問すること。
　d. 最高の顧客の所に立ち寄ること。

参考　I'd rather「むしろ～したい」がポイント。

66.　　　　　　　　　　　　　　　　　　　　　　　　b

訳　男性：パーソナル・チェックをここで現金化できますか。
　　女性：すみません，給料またはトラベラーズチェックのみ現金化しております。角を曲がった銀行で聞いてみてください。
　　男性：OK，どうも有難う。

Q 彼女のアドバイスは何ですか。
　a. 給料を現金に引き換えること。　b. 銀行に行くこと。
　c. 現金をチェックすること。　　　d. コーナーで待つこと。

参考　endorse「裏書する」　countersign a check「小切手に副署する」

Part III 会話問題　183

67.

Woman: The end of the fiscal year is coming up and the accountants are really busy.
Man: I know. I've been waiting for the customer balance sheets for over a week now. I think the company should hire some temporary staff to give them a hand.
Woman: I'm sure they'd appreciate it. They could use any help they can get.

Q What does the man suggest?

a. Hire some temporary help.
b. Give them a hand now.
c. Finish the balance sheets.
d. Wait for a week.

68.

Man: Could you please bring me another pillow?
Woman: Of course. Would you like anything else?
Man: Yes, maybe some more peanuts.

Q Where are they speaking?

a. On a plane.
b. At a hotel.
c. In a bedroom.
d. In a department store.

69.

Woman: Matt, you seem to be putting on a little weight lately?
Man: I know Cindy. I'm always sitting in front of my computer and never find the time to exercise.
Woman: You should try what I do. Every day, during lunch break, I work out in the company gym for 30 minutes.

Q What does she suggest?

a. Gaining weight.
b. Exercising.
c. Working less.
d. Taking more breaks.

67. a

訳 女性: 会計年度末になりますから、会計係の人達は本当に忙しいのです。
男性: 知っています。私は現在，顧客の貸借対照表を1週間以上も待っているのです。会社は臨時職員を雇って手伝わせるべきだと思います。
女性: きっと彼らは有難がりますよ。猫の手も借りたいでしょうから。

Q 男性は何を提案していますか。
　a. 臨時雇いを何人か雇う。　　b. 今，彼らに手を貸す。
　c. 貸借対照表を終える。　　　d. 1週間待つ。

参考 balance sheet「貸借対照表」　この他 time sheet「タイムカード」 sheet music「一枚刷りの楽譜」　fact sheet「データ表，事実記述」

68. 基礎知識問題 a

訳 男性: 枕をもう一つ持ってきてもらえますか。
女性: 承知いたしました。他に何かいりますか。
男性: はい，できればピーナッツをもう少しお願いします。

Q 彼らはどこで話しているのですか。
　a. 飛行機で。　　　　b. ホテルで。
　c. ベッドルームで。　d. デパートで。

参考 flight attendant と passenger の会話。

69. b

訳 女性: マット，あなたは最近少し太ってきたようね。
男性: わかっているよ，シンディー。私は常に私のコンピュータの前に座っていて運動をする時間がないのだよ。
女性: あなたも私みたいにするべきね。私は毎日，昼休みの時間に会社のジムで30分間トレーニングしているのよ。

Q 彼女は何を提案しているのですか。
　a. 体重を増やすこと。　　　b. 運動すること。
　c. 前より働かないこと。　　d. もっと休みをとること。

参考 女性の最後のコメントで解答が確定するが，冒頭ですでにどのような会話になるか内容が予測できる。

Part III 会話問題

70.

Woman: Tony, is it true that you're going overseas to supervise the installation of all the radar equipment we've sold?
Man: That's right. I'll be gone for three months and be on four continents. I just wish I could bring my family.
Woman: Well, at least you can always call every few days.

Q What does she suggest to Tony?

    a. To install some equipment.
    b. To bring his family.
    c. To stay a minimum of a few days.
    d. To telephone his family.

71.

Man: Charlene, I'd like to introduce you to Paul Martinez. He's a computer specialist from Mexico we just hired.
Woman: Nice to meet you. If you like, stop by my office and I can give you an organizational chart and a list of the facilities at this plant.
Man: That's very kind of you. I appreciate it.

Q What does she suggest?

    a. He come to her office.   b. He look at the facilities.
    c. It was nice to meet him.   d. He join the organization.

72.

Woman: Let's put the new coffee maker on the factory floor.
Man: I don't know if that's such a good idea. One of the forklifts from the shipping department might hit it. What about the employee lounge?
Woman: All right, let's do that, even though there's not much room there.

Q Where will they put the coffee maker?

    a. In the lunchroom.   b. In the employee lounge.
    c. In the shipping department.   d. On the factory floor.

70.   d

訳 女性: トニー，あなたは当社の販売した全レーダー設備の設置を監督しに外国に行かれるのは本当ですか。
男性: その通りです。3ヵ月間で4大陸に行きます。私の家族を連れていければ良いのですが。
女性: まあ，少なくとも，いつも2〜3日ごとに電話はできますね。

Q 彼女はトニーに何を提案しているのですか。
 a. 設備を設置すること。　　b. 彼の家族を連れてくること。
 c. 最低2，3日は滞在すること。　d. 彼の家族に電話をかけること。

参考 "I just wish I could〜"で男性が家族を連れて行けない事がわかる。

71.   a

訳 男性: シャーリーン，あなたをポール・マルティネスにご紹介したいと思います。メキシコから来たコンピュータ専門家で，入社したばかりです。
女性: お目にかかれて光栄です。もし良かったら私のオフィスに立ち寄ってください，この工場の組織図と設備リストを差し上げられます。
男性: ご親切にしていただきまして有難うございます。

Q 彼女は何を提案しているのですか。
 a. 彼が彼女のオフィスに来る。　b. 彼が設備を見る。
 c. 彼に会えて素晴らしかった。　d. 彼が組織に加わる。

参考 suggestのため選択肢a．b．d の動詞は仮定法現在形になっている。

72.   基礎知識問題   b

訳 女性: 新しいコーヒーメーカーを工場フロアに置きましょう。
男性: どうだろう。はたして良い考えかな。輸送部のフォークリフトがぶつかるかもしれない。従業員ラウンジはどうですか。
女性: そうね。そうしましょう。そこにはあまりスペースがありませんけれど。

Q 彼らはコーヒーメーカーをどこに置くのですか。
 a. 昼食部屋で。　　　　b. 従業員ラウンジに。
 c. 輸送部の中に。　　　d. 工場フロアに。

参考 人物Aの冒頭コメントに解答がある可能性が極めて低い。話の流れについていかれるかがポイント。

73.

Woman: Did you book a hotel room yet? Atlanta will be really crowded during the trade show.
Man: Yes, I arrive on the 13th and leave on the 19th. That should give me enough time to visit every exhibition. How about you?
Woman: I'm not going. I have to deliver a proposal in Zurich during that time.

Q Where is the trade show being held?

    a. At the Atlantic Hotel.   b. In a crowded exhibition center.
    c. In Atlanta.   d. In Zurich.

74.

Woman: Hold on. You can't go in there without a hard hat.
Man: Don't worry, I'm just going in for a minute to get my lunch box.
Woman: Sorry, regulations say that no one can enter without a hard hat.

Q Where does this conversation take place?

    a. In front of a restaurant.   b. Near a new office.
    c. Outside a factory.   d. At a park.

75.

Man: Laura, which area do you think has the best potential for our new discount store, downtown or the suburbs?
Woman: It's difficult to say. Downtown by the main station is good, but most of the major highways are in the suburbs.
Man: That's right. Besides, research has shown that land is too expensive for this type of store downtown.

Q Where will the new store probably be located?

    a. Downtown.   b. By the highway.
    c. In the suburbs.   d. Near the train station.

73.   c

訳 女性: もうホテルの部屋を予約しましたか。アトランタはトレード・ショーの間は本当に混みますよ。
男性: はい, 私は13日に到着して19日に出ます。それで全展示を見に行くのに十分時間があると思います。あなたはどうなさるのですか。
女性: 私は行きません。その時期にチューリッヒで提案を発表しなければならないのです。

Q トレード・ショーはどこで開催されますか。
  a. アトランティック・ホテルで。   b. 混雑した展示センターで。
  c. アトランタで。   d. チューリッヒで。

参考 冒頭の女性のコメントを聞いた瞬間に解答できれば次の設問を読む時間が出来る。瞬時の判断が出来るかどうかで点数に違いが出る。

74.   c

訳 女性: 待って。ヘルメット無しでそこに入ることはできないのよ。
男性: 心配はいらないよ。ちょっと弁当箱を取りに行くだけだから。
女性: 残念だけど, 規則でヘルメットを被っていない人は誰も入れないことになっているのよ。

Q この会話の場所はどこですか。
  a. レストランの前で。   b. 新しいオフィスの近く。
  c. 工場の外で。   d. 公園で。

参考 hard hat「ヘルメット」と言う単語を聞いて推測できる場所

75.   c

訳 男性: ローラ, 当社の新しい安売り店を設置するのに一番潜在性があるのは下町と郊外のどちらの地域だと思いますか。
女性: どちらと言い切るのは難しいですね。下町の主要駅の側が良いですが, 幹線道路のほとんどは郊外にありますからね。
男性: その通りです。それに調査によると, このタイプの店舗を下町に建てるには土地代が高すぎますね。

Q 新しい店の場所はどこになりますか。
  a. 下町   b. ハイウェイのそば
  c. 郊外   d. 駅に近い

参考 冒頭の長い疑問文を速解できることが第1条件。

Part III 会話問題

76.

Woman: I'm going to Dallas in a week for an interview with the director of admissions at the University of Texas.

Man: Good luck, Sue. How long do you think the entire process will take?

Woman: I don't know, but I've been preparing for three weeks. I just hope I don't get too nervous.

Q How long will Sue be in Dallas?

    a. She's not really sure.   b. For three weeks.

    c. It depends if the director likes her.   d. At least a week.

77.

Man: Do you want to buy or lease?

Woman: I'm not sure. Does a lease include maintenance and emergency road service?

Man: It only includes towing.

Q Where does this conversation take place?

    a. In a real estate agency.   b. At a distribution center.

    c. At a service station.   d. At an automobile dealership.

78.

Man: Reading your résumé I see that you have a degree in accounting.

Woman: That's correct. I specialized in taxes and investments.

Man: Actually, we're looking for someone with production management skills, but you're welcome to fill out an application anyway.

Q In which department are they speaking?

    a. The tax department.

    b. The accounting department.

    c. The personnel department.

    d. The production department.

76.　　　　　　　　　　　　　　　　　　　　　　　　　a

[訳] 女性: 私は1週間したらダラスに行って，テキサス大学の入学事務担当者の面接を受けます。
　　男性: ご幸運を，スー。全行程はどのくらいかかると思いますか。
　　女性: わかりません，でも3週間も準備したし，あまりあがらないように願っています。

[Q] スーはどのくらいダラスに滞在するのですか。
　a. はっきりとはわからない。　　　　b. 3週間。
　c. ディレクターが彼女が好きかによる。　d. 少なくとも1週間。

[参考] How longの質問であっても明確な解答があるとは限らない。

77.　　　　　　　　　　　　　　　　　　　　　　　　　d

[訳] 男性: ご購入ですかそれともリースですか。
　　女性: はっきりとは決めていません。リースはメンテナンスと非常事態用ロードサービスを含みますか。
　　男性: 牽引だけです。

[Q] この会話はどこでおこなわれていますか。
　a. 不動産屋で。　　　　　　　　　b. 流通センターで。
　c. サービス・ステーションで。　　d. 自動車ディーラーで。

[参考] maintenance, road service, towingで推量。distribution「分配，流通」

78.　　　　　　　　　　　　　　　　　　　　　　　　　c

[訳] 男性: あなたの履歴書によるとあなたは会計学の学位をもっていらっしゃるのですね！
　　女性: その通りです。専攻は税金と投資でした。
　　男性: 本当は生産管理技能を持った人を探しているのですが，あなたが応募用紙に記入してくださるのは歓迎です。

[Q] 彼らどの部で話しているのですか。
　a. 税務部　　　　　　　　　　　b. 会計部
　c. 人事部　　　　　　　　　　　d. 生産部

[参考] degree「学位，程度，度，度合い」

Part III 会話問題　191

79.

Man: Carol, do you know if the monthly sales report is in the file cabinet?

Woman: I'm not sure. The last time I saw it, it was on the assistant manager's desk.

Man: Now I remember. He left it next to the copy machine after reading it.

Q Where is the report?

    a. By the copier.   b. In the file cabinet.

    c. With the assistant manager.   d. On the coffee machine.

80.

Woman: There you go, Mr. Evans, I've checked the entire content of the presentation you're going to give next week.

Man: Thank you, Mrs. Kanemoto. What do you think?

Woman: My advice would be to start with the production figures first, and then go on to the research and sales budgets.

Q What does Mrs. Kanemoto suggest?

    a. To give the budgets first.

    b. To change the topic order.

    c. To give the presentation next week.

    d. To start production fast.

81.

Man: I'd like to rent a safety deposit box.

Woman: Could you tell me what you'll be keeping in it so I know the proper size?

Man: Just a few legal papers and some stock certificates.

Q Where does this conversation take place?

    a. In a rental shop.   b. In a bank.

    c. At a lawyer's office.   d. At a stock broker's office.

79. 基礎知識問題　　a

訳　男性: キャロル, 月次売上高報告がファイル・キャビネットの中にあるかどうか知っていますか。
　　女性: いいえ。それを最後に見た時は課長補佐の机の上にありました。
　　男性: ああ思い出した。彼はそれを読んだ後にコピー機のそばに置いていったのだ。

Q　レポートはどこですか。
　a. コピー機のそば。　　　　　b. ファイル・キャビネットの中。
　c. 課長補佐が持っている。　　d. コーヒー自動販売機の上。

参考　全文を聞いてから判断。assistant manager「係長, 課長補佐」

80.　　b

訳　女性: はい, どうぞ, エバンスさん。あなたが来週なさるプレゼンテーションの全内容をチェックしました。
　　男性: どうも有難うございます, 金本さん。あなたのお考えは？
　　女性: 私のアドバイスとしては, 最初に生産統計から始め, それから研究と販売予算に移っていくのがいいと思います。

Q　金本夫人は何を提案しているのですか。
　a. 最初に予算を出すこと。
　b. トピックの順番を変えること。
　c. 来週プレゼンテーションを行うこと。
　d. 生産を速く始めること。

参考　figure「数字, 図形」　figures「統計, データ」
　　　figure of speech「言葉のあや」

81.　　b

訳　男性: 貸金庫を賃借したいのです。
　　女性: 大きさは保管するものによりますが？
　　男性: 法律書類を2, 3枚と株券が数枚だけです。

Q　この会話はどこで行われていますか。
　a. レンタル店で。　　　　　b. 銀行で。
　c. 弁護士事務所で。　　　　d. 株式ブローカーの事務所で。

参考　貸金庫がある場所は主に銀行とホテル。

Part III　会話問題

82.

Woman: The sales manager just told me he's going to transfer me to the new Denver store.
Man: I heard Denver is a pretty nice city: clean air, friendly people, and very close to the ski resorts.
Woman: I know, but I'm most concerned about the schools since my children are still young.

Q Where are the ski slopes located?
   a. A short trip from Vancouver.   b. Quite near the city.
   c. Close to his children's school. d. By the manager's office.

83.

Man: At the rate the company is growing we're going to need both more office and production space soon.
Woman: How long do you think we can stay in our present premises?
Man: Management has to decide to move into a new building or expand this one within a year.

Q How long can the company stay in its present facilities?
   a. Till the manager buys the office.   b. For less than a year.
   c. Until the company stops growing.   d. For the time being.

84.

Man: Yes, I have a question. How long are the vacations with this company?
Woman: It depends on how long you've been here. You start with two weeks. After five years, three weeks. After ten years, vacation time is based on your sales performance.
Man: I see. Can I fill out an application?

Q How much vacation time does a new employee begin with?
   a. Two weeks.   b. Three weeks.
   c. Four weeks.   d. Five weeks.

82.　　　　　　　　　　　　　　　　　　　　　　　b

訳　女性：営業部長がちょっと私に話してくれたのですが、私はデンバーの新店舗へ転勤になるそうです。
　　男性：聞くところによるとデンバーは非常に素晴らしい都市だそうですよ。空気は汚れていないし、人々はフレンドリー、それに、ごく近くにスキーリゾートがあるとのことです。
　　女性：そうなのですが、子供たちが幼いので学校の事が一番心配です。

Q　スキー場はどこですか。
　　a. バンクーバーから小旅行で行ける所。　b. 都市にかなり近い。
　　c. 彼の子供の学校に近い。　　　　　　　d. マネージャーの事務所の近く。

参考　DenverはColorado州にあり、Vancouverはカナダにある。

83.　　　　　　　　　　　　　　　　　　　　　　　b

訳　男性：この割合で会社が成長していくと、すぐにオフィスと生産スペースの両方をもっと大きくする必要がでてきます。
　　女性：現在の施設にいられるのはどのくらいだと思いますか。
　　男性：経営陣は新しい建物へ引っ越すか、これを広げるかを一年以内に決めなければなりません。

Q　会社はどのくらいの間現在の施設に留まることができますか。
　　a. マネージャーが事務所を買うまで。　b. 1年未満。
　　c. 会社の成長が止まるまで。　　　　　d. 当分の間

参考　a.c.dの事項は言及されていない。
　　　premise(s)「建物、施設、敷地、構内」

84.　基礎知識問題　　　　　　　　　　　　　　　　　a

訳　男性：はい、質問があります。この会社の休暇はどのくらいですか。
　　女性：それは勤続年数によります。最初は2週間。5年経つと3週間。10年以上は販売業績に基づいて休暇の長さが決まります。
　　男性：わかりました。応募用紙に記入していいですか。

Q　新人雇用者の休暇はどのくらいからになりますか。
　　a. 2週間。　　　　　　　　　　b. 3週間。
　　c. 4週間。　　　　　　　　　　d. 5週間。

参考　数字は聞いた瞬間に理解できるように集中的に練習すること。

85.

Man: Does anyone have the second proposal from the Sherman Plastics Company?
Woman: We haven't gotten it yet, but I'll check the mail as soon as it comes in.
Man: OK. It generally comes in before lunchtime.

Q At what time does the mail usually come?

a. Soon.
b. After lunchtime.
c. At 2:00 p.m.
d. In the morning.

86.

Woman: Sorry, I don't have time for coffee. I have to be at the safety meeting in ten minutes.
Man: Well it's 11:35 now. Where is the meeting?
Woman: On the factory floor but I have to stop by the storage room first to pick up a hard hat.

Q At what time does the meeting start?

a. At ten minutes to eleven.
b. At 11:45.
c. Before she gets any coffee.
d. When she gets to the factory floor.

87.

Man: Sharon, do you have a few minutes to check the outstanding balance for the Flores Foods account?
Woman: Frankly Jeff I don't, but I'm free anytime tomorrow.
Man: All right. Meet me tomorrow in the law library. I'll be there between two and four o'clock doing research.

Q When can Sharon meet Jeff?

a. In a few minutes.
b. As soon as Frank leaves.
c. Tomorrow in the law library.
d. The day after tomorrow.

	解答

85. 基礎知識問題   d

訳 男性: 誰かシャーマン・プラスチック社から来た2番目の提案を持っていますか。
女性: まだそれを受け取っていませんが郵便が着き次第チェックします。
男性: OK, たいてい昼食時間前に来ますよ。

Q 郵便は通常何時に届きますか。

  a. すぐに   b. 昼食後
  c. 2時に   d. 午前に

参考 mail clerk「郵便局員」 postage「郵便料金, 送料」

86.   b

訳 女性: 残念ですがコーヒーをいただく時間がありません。10分したら安全会議に出席しなければなりません。
男性: ええと, 今は11時35分です。会議はどこで行われるのですか。
女性: 工場のフロアでですが, その前に倉庫に寄ってヘルメットを持っていかなくてはなりません。

Q 会議は何時に始まりますか。

  a. 11時10分前に。   b. 11時45分に。
  c. 彼女がコーヒーを取る前。   d. 彼女が工場のフロアに着いたとき。

参考 in ten minutes「10分したら」 within 10 minutes「10分以内に」

87.   c

訳 男性: シャロン, フローレス・フード社の未払いをチェックするのにちょっと時間がありますか。
女性: 実のところ, ジェフ, だめなのです, でも明日ならいつでもいいですよ。
男性: わかりました。明日, 法律図書館で会いましょう。2時から4時の間, そこで調査しています。

Q シャロンはいつジェフに会うことができますか。

  a. 数分で。   b. フランクが去ったらすぐ。
  c. 明日, 法律図書館で。   d. 明後日。

参考 a week from today「来週の今日」という表現もついでに覚えよう。

Part III 会話問題

88.

Woman: Hello, I'd like to order a limousine. Have it in front of the Parkside Hotel at 7:15 sharp.
Man: Of course, Ma'am. We'll have it there by seven o'clock. Can I ask how long you'll be needing it for?
Woman: I'm not exactly sure. I'm taking some clients to dinner and a show.

Q At what time does she want the limousine?
    a. At exactly 7 o'clock.   b. At 7:10.
    c. At 7:15.   d. At 7:45.

89.

Man: Kyoko, I thought you were coming skiing with us this weekend?
Woman: Sorry, I can't. I was out sick on Tuesday and Wednesday, so I have to come in and finish that cost analysis report I've been working on.
Man: That's too bad. I hope you'll be able to come with us on the next trip in two weeks.

Q Why is the woman working?
    a. So she can go skiing.
    b. Because she missed some days.
    c. So she will be free in two weeks.
    d. Because she had a long vacation.

90.

Woman: Tom, I e-mailed the revised report to the auditing department.
Man: Great, Helen. Did you also include the new tax figures?
Woman: The accounting department said they wouldn't have them prepared until late this afternoon.

Q Why didn't she send the tax figures?
    a. Helen couldn't find the report.
    b. The e-mail system is being revised.
    c. The auditing department opens this afternoon.
    d. They're not finished yet.

88. 基礎知識問題 　　　　　　　　　　　　　　　　c

訳 女性: こんにちは，リムジンをお願いします。7時15分ちょうどにパークサイド・ホテルの前でそれを待たせておいてください。
男性: かしこまりました奥様，そこに7時までに行かせておきます。どれくらいの間ご入用ですか。
女性: はっきりとはわかりません。お客様方を夕食とショーにお連れします。

Q 彼女は何時にリムジンが欲しいのですか。
　a. ちょうど7時。　　　　　　b. 7時10分。
　c. 7時15分。　　　　　　　 d. 7時45分。

参考 女性は7時15分と頼んでいる。

89. 　　　　　　　　　　　　　　　　　　　　　b

訳 男性: 京子さん，今週末は我々と一緒にスキーに行くと思っていましたが？
女性: ごめんなさい。だめになりました，私は火曜と水曜に病欠しましたので，出社してずっと取り組んでいたコスト分析報告を終えなければならないのです。
男性: それは残念。2週間後にする次回の旅行では私たちと一緒に来られることを願っていますよ。

Q なぜ女性は働いているのですか。
　a. 彼女はスキーに行けるように。　　b. 彼女が数日間休んだから。
　c. 彼女は2週間したら自由になるように。 d. 彼女が長期の休暇をとったから。

参考 be out「仕事を休んで」

90. 　　　　　　　　　　　　　　　　　　　　　d

訳 女性: トム，会計検査部に修正済みレポートを電子メールで送りましたよ。
男性: ヘレン，素晴らしい。新しい税金の計算を入れましたか。
女性: 会計部によると今日の午後遅くまで準備できないとのことでした。

Q なぜ，彼女は税金計算を送らなかったのですか。
　a. ヘレンはそのレポートを見つけることができませんでした。
　b. 電子メール・システムは修正されているところです。
　c. 会計検査部は今日の午後に開きます。
　d. まだ終わっていないので。

参考 audit (accounts)「会計検査をする，監査する」　auditor「監査役」

91.

Man: Have a good weekend. I'll be here catching up on some work.
Woman: Again. You seem to spend almost every weekend at the office working!
Man: I know, but since my promotion to section manager the president has been giving me a lot of extra paperwork, and I can't refuse.

Q Why will the man be at the office?
   a. He can't spend time with his family.
   b. He now has more responsibilities.
   c. The president doesn't like him.
   d. Because he enjoys doing paperwork.

92.

Woman: Jack, can you arrange for a taxi to pick us up at 10?
Man: I think that's too late. We should leave earlier if we want to get to the airport for our 12:30 flight.
Woman: It shouldn't be a problem; rush hour is over by about 9:20, so traffic should be light.

Q When are they going to leave for the airport?
   a. By 9:20.   b. At 10 o'clock.   c. After 12:30.   d. Early.

93.

Woman: Have you heard that the manager fired Paul Kelly yesterday?
Man: Are you sure? He was one of the most conscientious employees in the company.
Woman: I know. I think he must have done something to anger one of the higher-ups.

Q Why did Mr. Kelly lose his job?
   a. He started a fire in the company.
   b. He was angry at an employee.
   c. An executive didn't like him.
   d. He wasn't a very good worker.

91. **b**

訳 男性: 楽しい週末を。私はここで仕事の遅れを取り戻します。
女性: またですか、ほとんど毎週末オフィスで働いているようですね！
男性: そうなのですよ。でも私が課長に昇進してから、社長が今まで以上に文書業務をたくさんよこすし、私は断れないのです。

Q なぜ、男性はオフィスにいるのですか。
a. 彼は彼の家族と共に時を過ごせない。
b. 現在、彼の職務はより重くなっている。
c. 社長は彼が好きではない。
d. 彼は文書業務を楽しんでするからです。

参考 promotion「昇進」 responsibility「職務, 責務」

92. 基礎知識問題 **b**

訳 女性: ジャック、タクシーに10時に迎えに来るように手配してくださる？
男性: それでは遅すぎると思います。12:30の便に間に合うよう空港に着きたいのならもっと速く出るべきです。
女性: それは問題ではありません、9時20分までにラッシュアワーは済んでいますから、交通量は少ないはずです。

Q 彼らはいつ空港に向けて出発するつもりですか。
a. 9時20分まで。 b. 10時に。 c. 12時30分以降に。 d. 早く。

参考 traffic congestion「交通渋滞」

93. **c**

訳 女性: マネージャーが昨日ポール・ケリーを解雇したのを聞いていますか。
男性: 確かですか。彼は会社で最も良心的な従業員の1人でした。
女性: そうですね。彼は上役のだれかを怒らせるようなことをしたのにちがいないと思います。

Q なぜ、ケリー氏は職を失ったのですか。
a. 彼は会社で火事を起こしました。
b. 彼は従業員の1人に怒っていました。
c. 重役が彼を好きではなかった。
d. 彼はあまり良い労働者ではなかった。

参考 conscientious「良心的な」 high-up「上司, お偉方, 幹部」

94.

Man: I usually find time to play tennis every other weekend.
Woman: How long have you been playing?
Man: Let's see. I started when I was about nine, so for about 20 years now.

Q How often does he play tennis?
   a. Every week.
   b. Twice a month.
   c. On the weekends.
   d. Daily since he was nine years old.

95.

Man: Merrill, were you able to get any work done on the flight from Montreal?
Woman: No, Evan, because when we took off, I dropped my personal computer and it wouldn't start up.
Man: That's a shame. I was hoping you could have finished the figures for the Brisco Pipe deal before you got back.

Q Why couldn't she finish the figures?
   a. Her PC wouldn't function.
   b. It was a rough take-off.
   c. Her PC was not allowed on board.
   d. The flight was too short.

96.

Woman: Isn't today the day the production department is scheduled to give its monthly report?
Man: No, it's not due until the 14th. By the way, I heard a rumor that they're going to try to justify the cost effectiveness of all that new equipment they've been buying recently.
Woman: I've heard that too. I've heard they're having some labor problems as well.

Q Why is there no monthly report today?
   a. There are some labor problems.
   b. It's not the right day.
   c. It isn't justified yet.
   d. They are buying new equipment.

94. 基礎知識問題　　　　　　　　　　　　　　　　　　　　b

訳　男性：私は通常，隔週末にテニスをする時間を見つけます。
　　女性：あなたはどのくらいプレーをしているのですか。
　　男性：ええと，わたしが9歳くらいの時からプレーを始めたので現在で20年くらいになります。

Q　彼はどれくらいの頻度でテニスをするのですか。
　a. 毎週。　　b. 月に2回。　　c. 週末に。　　d. 9才の時から毎日。

参考　How long have you been playing? と設問の違いに気をつける。

95.　　　　　　　　　　　　　　　　　　　　　　　　　　a

訳　男性：メリル，モントリオールからの便では仕事ができましたか。
　　女性：いいえ，エヴァン，飛び立った時に私のパソコンを落としてしまったので全然作動しなかったのです。
　　男性：それは残念。あなたが戻る前に，ブリスコ・パイプ取引の計算を終わって下さっていればいいのにと願っていたのです。

Q　なぜ，彼女は計算を終えることができなかったのですか。
　a. 彼女のコンピュータが機能しなかった。
　b. その離陸が乱暴だった。
　c. 彼女はPCを機上持込出来なかった。
　d. フライトが短すぎた。

参考　start up a computer　コンピュータを始動させる

96.　　　　　　　　　　　　　　　　　　　　　　　　　　b

訳　女性：今日は生産部が月報を出す予定日ではないですか。
　　男性：いいえ14日が提出期限です。ところで，生産部が最近自分たちの購入した全ての新設備のコストパフォーマンスを正当化しようとしているといううわさを耳にしました。
　　女性：私もです。彼らが何か労働問題を抱えているとも聞いています。

Q　なぜ，今日は月報がないのですか。
　a. 労働問題が若干ある。　　　　b. 正しい日ではない。
　c. それはまだ正当化されていない。d. 彼らは新しい設備を買っている。

参考　"By the way" で本論から話しの流れが変わる。
　　　cost efficiency「費用効率」を覚えよう。　　justify「正当化する」

97.

Woman: What's wrong with our concrete supplier? I've been calling them all day about the price increase but can't get a straight answer.

Man: The usual salesman we deal with there has retired. Why don't you have your assistant go over and find out who's in charge now.

Woman: Good idea. I really need a price update for the construction estimate I'm working on.

Q Why is her assistant going to the supplier?

 a. To complain about the price of concrete.
 b. To talk to the retired salesman.
 c. For a construction estimate.
 d. To find out who the new representative is.

98.

Woman: It took Carlos five hours to revise that contract last night.

Man: It doesn't surprise me; contracts are not one of Carlos' strong points.

Woman: That may be true, but he's very good with export documentation.

Q Why did it take Carlos so long to finish?

 a. He was working on some export papers.
 b. Because he's not strong enough.
 c. He's not an expert in that field.
 d. It took him five hours.

97.

解答 **d**

訳 女性: 当社のコンクリートの納入業者はどうかしたのですか。私は，あの価格上昇について話すために彼らに一日中電話をかけているのですが，きちんとした答えを得ることができません。
男性: いつも取引をしていたセールスマンが引退したのです。あなたのアシスタントを遣って，誰が現在担当なのか調べたらいかがですか。
女性: そうですね。抱えている建築の見積もりを出すのに最新の価格が本当に必要なのです。

Q なぜ，彼女のアシスタントは納入業者へ行くのですか。
 a. コンクリートの価格について不平を言うために。
 b. 引退したセールスマンと話すために。
 c. 建設見積もりのために。
 d. 新しい営業が誰であるか調べるために。

- -

参考 representative= sales representative「営業，販売員」

98.

解答 **c**

訳 女性: 昨晩カルロスがあの契約を修正するのに5時間かかりました。
男性: それには驚きません ― 契約はカルロスの得意なものの1つではありません。
女性: それは事実かもしれませんが，彼は輸出の書類作成がとてもうまいのです。

Q なぜ，カルロスは終わるのに長時間かかったのですか。
 a. 彼は輸出書類に取り掛かっていた。
 b. 彼が十分に強くないから。
 c. 彼はその分野の専門家ではない。
 d. それは5時間かかった。

- -

参考 strong point「得意な点，長所」
 documentation「書類化，書類作成」

Part III 会話問題 205

99.

Man: This meeting is really important. Our section is going to give the details on the stock dividends.

Woman: I won't be able to go, Bill. I just got a last-minute batch of new orders that have to be processed.

Man: That's more important. I'll take notes and let you know what happened after lunch.

Q Why can't the woman make the meeting?

a. She was ordered not to.
b. She has a lot of paperwork.
c. Because Bill will take notes.
d. She's going to proceed.

100.

Woman: That was an interesting seminar. I'm glad I attended, but I have to get going now.

Man: It's too bad you have to leave so soon. There's going to be a reception in about 30 minutes in the lounge.

Woman: I understand, but I have a long drive home and I want to get back before dark.

Q Why is she leaving?

a. She wants to get home before dark.
b. Thirty minutes is too long.
c. She hates parties.
d. The seminar wasn't so interesting.

99.

b

訳 男性: この会議は本当に重要です。我々のセクションは株式配当に関する詳細を発表します。
女性: 私は行けません，ビル。処理しなければならない新しいオーダーの一群をついさっき受け取ったところです。
男性: そのほうが重要ですね。私はメモを取って，どのような事が起こったのかを昼食後にお知らせしますよ。

Q なぜ，女性は会議に出席できないのですか。
 a. 彼女がしないように命令された。
 b. 彼女は書類仕事がたくさんある。
 c. ビルがノートを取るから。
 d. 彼女は進む。

・・・・・・・・・・・・・・・・・・・・・・・・・・・・・・・・

参考 dividend「配当」　batch「一まとまりの数量，束,一団，群」
process「書類などを処理する」
paperwork「事務処理，書類仕事」
take notes「ノートを取る，メモを取る」

100.

a

訳 女性: あれは面白いセミナーでしたね，出席して良かったわ。でも行かなければなりません。
男性: こんなに早く出発しなければならないとは残念です。30分くらいしたらラウンジでレセプションがあるのですよ。
女性: ええ。でも家へ帰るのに長く運転しなければなりませんし，日が暮れる前に戻りたいのです。

Q 彼女はどうして去ろうとしているのですか。
 a. 暗くなる前に家に戻りたい。
 b. 30分は，あまりに長い。
 c. 彼女はパーティーが大嫌いだ。
 d. セミナーはそれほど面白くなかった。

・・・・・・・・・・・・・・・・・・・・・・・・・・・・・・・・

参考 女性の最初のコメントで全体の背景説明をし，男性が現在の状況を述べています。更にそれに対して女性が応答し解答が得られるパターンです。

Part IV 説明文問題の攻略法

A フォーマット

Part IV は説明文問題です。1つの説明文に対して複数の設問（2〜4）があります。設問数は20ですから，説明文は7から8くらいとなります。文章が読まれるスピードは1分間に170語程度です。35秒くらいのパッセージを聴いて内容を記憶する練習をします。

Part IV 全体の長さは10分弱です。

B 問題の提示

Part IV の指示文　34秒
↓
問題開始
Questions 81 and 82 are based on the following speech.　4秒
↓（1秒）
問題文　（平均34秒で読まれる）
↓（1秒）
設問を読んで解答するように
Now read question 81 in your test book and answer it.（4秒）
↓（6秒）
設問を読んで解答するように
Now read question 82 in your test book and answer it.（4秒）
↓（8秒）
次の問題開始
Questions 83 and 84 are based on the following speech.

C 解答のコツ

Part III が終わった瞬間にこのパートの設問を2〜4題読むこと，これによって最初の説明文の設問が2題なのか，3題なのか見当がつ

きます。
　前もって設問が読めない人は，TOEICのPart I 説明文と導入部，また終了時からPart IIの指示文の中ごろまでの半端な時間を利用してPart IVの設問をざっと見ておくとよいでしょう。説明文を聴きながら解答できるようになることが目標です。解答できないものには時間をかけないことが重要です。

D 傾向と対策

　ここは最も難しいパートです。長文をスラッシュを書き入れながら読み速読速解の練習を行います。問題集でまずパターンを知り，ビジネス関係の語彙に慣れます。
　本試験では説明文中の情報提示と設問が同じ順序になっていない場合が一度くらいあるかもしれません。
　スコアが470点以下の場合は問題集で語彙のチェックと場面設定の会話，基本パターンの音読とシャドウィングを行います。470点以上の場合はビジネス英語の番組なども基礎知識の増強に利用します。特に730点突破を狙う場合は時事素材やネイティブ向けに書かれた一般雑誌，またTVや映画などいろいろなものを教材として使用します。ネイティブ用に書かれた記事を初見で1分あたり170語の速さで黙読し，その内容が大体つかめるように目指します。
　Part IVがウィーク・ポイントの場合は，聞きながら読んだり，メモを取る練習をして，集中力をうまく配分するスキルを磨く必要があります。

■ 問題パターンの分析

（1）社内放送
　　Who is Chris Benoit?　　注意！ 役職，仕事を答える。
　　Who is making this announcement?
　　　　　　　　　　　　　注意！ 告知している人の名前か役職
　　What is NOT true about it?
　　When did the negotiations start?　　注意！ 時間を答える。
　　What were the negotiations about?
　　How long will the seminar last?
　　What is the advantage of the product?　　注意！ 利点を指摘する。

(2) 店内放送
　　How long will the sale last?
　　Where does the event take place?
　　What is on sale?　　注意! セールの対象品は何かを答える。
　　What is suggested that the shoppers do?
　　Where is this announcement being given?

(3) 録音されたアナウンス / 電話
　　What is the caller asked to do?
　　Why is this announcement being given?
　　Why did the caller receive this message?
　　Why is the man calling?
　　What day is the museum closed?

(4) スピーチ紹介
　　Who is Steve Regal?　　注意! 役職を答える。
　　Who is the speaker?　　注意! 名前または役職を答える。
　　What does Mr. Bigelow talk about?

(5) 天気予報
　　What kind of weather is predicted?
　　What is the forecast for tomorrow?

(6) 交通情報 / 機内放送 / 空港のアナウンス
　　Why was the flight canceled?
　　When is the next flight to New York?
　　Where are the passengers supposed to go?
　　What is causing the delay?

(7) 広告 / 公共のお知らせ
　　Who would probably be most interested in buying the item?
　　What is being advertised?　　注意! よく出るので広告されている物は忘れないこと。
　　What kind of service is being advertised?
　　What is available at the shop?
　　Which product feature is introduced?　　注意! 製品の特徴を答える。
　　What day is the art gallery closed?
　　What is being predicted?
　　What is the purpose of the event?

練習問題 1—40

説明文を聞き，それに関する複数の設問に答えてください。 解答→p.218

Part IV

1.   2-37

Why should customers hurry?
- a. To be able to buy what they want.
- b. There aren't enough items.
- c. Because of their patronage.
- d. The sale is on the second floor.

2.

What is not on sale?
- a. Floppy disks.
- b. Printers.
- c. Software.
- d. Cables.

3.   2-38

How is traffic moving out of the city?
- a. Congested.
- b. Clear all the way.
- c. Steadily but slowly.
- d. Very smoothly.

4.

How often does this report take place?
- a. Every hour.
- b. Every 30 minutes.
- c. Every 20 minutes.
- d. Every 10 minutes.

5.   2-39

Who is the speaker addressing?
- a. Newly promoted managers.
- b. The weekly departmental meeting.
- c. Important decision makers.
- d. New department members.

6.

How should decisions be made?
- a. By the entire company.
- b. With thought and care.
- c. Through implementation.
- d. To the staff members.

Part IV 説明文問題

7. ──────────────── 2-40

Why are some employees staying?
- a. To unplug the electrical equipment.
- b. Only overnight.
- c. In case of emergencies.
- d. Because of flooding.

8.

What should employees do before leaving?
- a. Leave immediately.
- b. Drive safely.
- c. Close the office early.
- d. Turn off their computers.

9. ──────────────── 2-41

What is this story mostly about?
- a. Bond yields.
- b. A feasibility study.
- c. Percentage speculation.
- d. A feature story.

10.

Why will the market be closed?
- a. Because of the political situation.
- b. Because of a national holiday.
- c. Because trading was halted.
- d. Because bond futures fell.

11.

What is the new yield for Gold Star bonds?
- a. 0.7%
- b. 128.3
- c. 1.43%
- d. 0.3%

12. ──────────────── 2-42

Who can call Ritter and Associates?
- a. Satisfied clients.
- b. Consultants.
- c. Professionals.
- d. Any individual.

13.
What are Ritter and Associates' primary services?
  a. Securities trading.   b. Accounting.
  c. Loans.   d. Issuing bonds.

14.
Which markets does Ritter not deal in?
  a. Currency.   b. Real estate.
  c. Bonds.   d. Stocks.

15.   2-43
Why are the employees getting extra bonus money?
  a. Due to the hard work of the entire company.
  b. The president is generous.
  c. All departments contributed equally.
  d. Due to the high sales volume.

16.
Who will get stock options?
  a. Workers who sold over 17%.   b. The entire field staff.
  c. Managers and executives.   d. All white collar workers.

17.
What happened to last year's sales goal?
  a. It was 15%.
  b. A staff member made assertive efforts.
  c. Its objective was 17% lower.
  d. It was increased by 17%.

18.   2-44
What do you get if you subscribe before July 15th?
  a. A free book and a video.   b. 12 issues.
  c. A free book.   d. An aerobics video.

19.
How should you not pay?
  a. Money order.   b. Cash.
  c. Credit card.   d. Check.

20.
How long is the subscription for?
  a. Until July 15th.   b. Twenty-three weeks.
  c. A year.   d. Until you cancel.

21. ──────────────── 2-45
What was the biggest problem?
  a. Problems among workers. b. Money.
  c. Job dissatisfaction.   d. Running an office.

22.
When was the survey conducted?
  a. Previously.   b. A short time ago.
  c. Eight years ago.   d. In 1986.

23.
How many people were surveyed ?
  a. 86 percent.   b. Executives and office managers.
  c. Several hundred.   d. All of the Florida Chamber of Commerce.

24. ──────────────── 2-46
Why should the make, model and year be written?
  a. For the dealers.   b. So the car can be returned.
  c. To eliminate models. d. To make things go faster.

25.
What should customers do first?
  a. Take a number.   b. State the problem.
  c. Fill out the form.   d. Take a pen.

26.
Who will be served first?
- a. The one with the newest model.
- b. The one with the lowest number.
- c. Whoever came to the garage.
- d. The one with the biggest problem.

27. 2-47
What will happen on Friday?
- a. Winter will start.
- b. The rain will continue.
- c. It will clear up.
- d. It will be gloomy.

28.
What is "just around the corner?"
- a. The news.
- b. A good forecast.
- c. Warm weather.
- d. Winter.

29.
What's the weather like now?
- a. Raining.
- b. High pressure.
- c. A little damp.
- d. Clearing.

30. 2-48
What do the rates not include?
- a. Breakfast.
- b. Meeting rooms.
- c. Limousine service.
- d. Valet parking.

31.
What is a good reason for a businessman to stay at this hotel?
- a. Sydney is a beautiful city.
- b. Breakfast is free.
- c. Its proximity to the financial section.
- d. Reasonable charge for the sports facilities.

32.
How can you get the best rates?
 a. Pay by company voucher. b. Stay for only one day.
 c. Stay in connecting rooms. d. Use a company credit card.

33.
Who would probably not stay here?
 a. Honeymooners. b. Executives.
 c. Sales people. d. Managers.

34. ──────────────── 2-49
What is the main topic of the presentation?
 a. Hotel management. b. Banquet arrangements.
 c. A Luncheon meeting. d. Restaurant service.

35.
What should servers regard themselves as at all times?
 a. Employees. b. Managers.
 c. Professionals. d. charming.

36.
Who is the speaker at this presentation?
 a. A waitress. b. A chef.
 c. A caterer. d. None of these.

37. ──────────────── 2-50
What can be said about the 400 employees?
 a. They will all be retrained. b. They will not lose their jobs.
 c. They need to be alarmed. d. No one will be hired.

38.
Why were the new machines installed?
- a. Because they are more cost effective.
- b. Due to the moratorium.
- c. So they can operate on a limited basis.
- d. Because of the new project.

39.
When will the company hire new employees?
- a. When they run efficiently.
- b. Next June.
- c. When they are fully trained.
- d. After a few years.

40.
What are current employees encouraged to do?
- a. Get advice from their supervisors.
- b. Resign at once to get a bonus.
- c. Look for a new job.
- d. Get training to operate the robots.

文章を意味のまとまりごとにスラッシュで区切り理解する練習です。設問1から設問6までは、文章を冒頭から素早く理解するための練習のスラッシュ・リーディングの参考例にもなっています。

Part IV Scripts

Questions 1 — 2 refer to the following announcement.

Attention all customers:/ Right now/ all computer related items/ such as disks, software, carrying cases, cables, and so on,/ are being offered/ at a 60% discount./ This is/ an extra discount/ from our usual everyday low prices./

The sale is on the second floor/ and does not include/ any electronic hardware.// Now is your chance /to save over half/ on hundreds of items.//This sale will only last /until 6:30/ so hurry/ before inventory runs out.// We periodically offer you /these sales/ to thank you/ for your patronage.//   (88 words)

1.

Why should customers hurry?
- a. To be able to buy what they want.
- b. There aren't enough items.
- c. Because of their patronage.
- d. The sale is on the second floor.

2.

What is not on sale?
- a. Floppy disks.
- b. Printers.
- c. Software.
- d. Cables.

> スラッシュを記入する箇所は各々の文章判断によって異なります。目標は文脈を正確に瞬時に捉えることです。練習方法がわからない時はテープ中のネイティブの読みを聞きながら，息継ぎの個所でスラッシュを書き入れます。

スクリプト 訳

設問 1―2 は，以下の告知に関するものです。

お客様にお知らせいたします。ただ今，ディスク，ソフトウェア，キャリングケース，ケーブルなどコンピュータ関係の全品が，6割引で提供されております。これは，通常の廉価からさらに値引きしたものです。セールは2階で行われており，電子ハードウェアは含まれておりません。現在，5割以上のお得な割引が何百品もございます。このセールは在庫がなくなる前の6時30分までのみのものですのでお急ぎください。当社は皆さまのご愛顧に対する御礼として定期的に当セールを提供いたしております。

解答

1.　　　　　　　　　　　　　　　　　　　　　　　　　　a

訳　お客さまたちはどうして急ぐべきなのですか。

- a. 買いたいものを買うため。
- b. 品物が十分ない。
- c. 彼らの愛顧のため。
- d. セールは2階でやっている。

参考　6行目にセールは在庫がなくなる前の6時30分までのものとある。

2.　　　　　　　　　　　　　　　　　　　　　　　　　　b

訳　セールになっていないものは何ですか。

- a. フロッピー・ディスク。
- b. プリンター。
- c. ソフトウェア。
- d. ケーブル。

参考　列挙されたものを覚えておくのは以外と難しい。この種の問題は問題文を聞きながら解答するように予め注意しておく必要がある。

Questions 3 — 4 refer to the following traffic report.

Good evening ladies and gentlemen,/ this is the WATB Traffic Report.// We have /a pretty clear view of the city/ from our traffic helicopter tonight.// Rush hour began/ only about 20 minutes ago.// Nothing major to report so far./ Traffic is moving/ a little slowly but steadily/ in the outbound lanes.// And we have/ a report of minor delays/ in the area of the Southside Mall/ due to a fire at noon/ but nothing to worry about.// That's it for now.// See you/ in another ten minutes/ with another update.//   (89 words)

3.

How is traffic moving out of the city?
- a. Congested.
- b. Clear all the way.
- c. Steadily but slowly.
- d. Very smoothly.

4.

How often does this report take place?
- a. Every hour.
- b. Every 30 minutes.
- c. Every 20 minutes.
- d. Every 10 minutes.

設問 3 — 4 は，以下の交通情報に関するものです。

　今晩は皆さん，こちらはWATB交通情報です。今夜は私どもの交通ヘリコプターから都市がかなり鮮明に見えます。今までのところ大きく変わった情報はありません。市外行きの車線はややのろのろとしていますが，着実に流れております。ラッシュアワーは20分前に始まったばかりです。また，正午に起こった火事のためにサウスサイド・モールでは少々渋滞とのことですが，心配はご無用です。それでは，また10分したら新しい情報をお知らせします。

|解答|

3.   c

訳 市から出ていく交通はどうですか。
- a. 渋滞している。
- b. 全線にわたって空いている。
- c. 着実だがのろのろ。
- d. とてもスムーズ。

参考 a little slowly but steadily in the outbound lanes と述べられている。

4.   d

訳 この情報はどのくらいの頻度で聞けますか。
- a. 1時間ごと。
- b. 30分間ごと。
- c. 20分ごと。
- d. 10分ごと。

参考 「あと10分したら」という事から10分毎だとわかる。

Questions 5 — 6 refer to the following business talk.

Thank you for coming./ As new department heads,/ you will find/ that some of your most important and complex duties/ will include /scheduling, meeting production deadlines, handling personnel problems,/ and dealing with/ higher management.// Great care and thought/ must be given/ to your decisions/ and your methods of implementing them. // The decisions/ you make/ will not only affect your particular departments,/ but sometimes the entire company as well.// I advise you/ to always be available /to your subordinates/ if they have/ any questions or problems.// My congratulations again/ on your promotions,/ and the best of luck to you all.//   (98 words)

5.

Who is the speaker addressing?
- a. Newly promoted managers.
- b. The weekly departmental meeting.
- c. Important decision makers.
- d. New department members.

6.

How should decisions be made?
- a. By the entire company.
- b. With thought and care.
- c. Through implementation.
- d. To the staff members.

設問 5 — 6 は，以下の商談に関するものです。
　お出でいただき有難うございます。新任の部長として，諸君は自分の重要かつ複雑な義務のなかにはスケジューリング，生産期限に間に合うこと，人事問題の取り扱い，そして，経営上層部に対処することが含まれていることがわかるでしょう。諸君の決定と，その実行には甚大な注意と熟考を払わなければなりません。諸君の決定は，諸君の部だけではなく，時によっては会社全体に影響を及ぼします。もし諸君の部下が質問や問題を持っている場合，常に対応ができるようにしているよう勧めます。諸君の昇進を再度お祝いするとともに，最上のご幸運を祈っています。

|解答|

5.   a
|訳| スピーカーは誰に話しているのですか。
　a. 最近昇進して部長になった人達。　b. 毎週の部門会議。
　c. 重要な意思決定者。　　　　　　　d. 部門の新しいメンバー。

|参考| new department heads の人たちに，その心構えについて話をしているのがわかる。

6.   b
|訳| 決定はどのようになされなるべきですか。
　a. 会社全体で。　　　　　b. 考慮と注意をもって。
　c. 実施によって。　　　　d. 社員に。

|参考| Great care and thought must be given to your decisions とある。

Part IV 説明文問題　223

Questions 7 — 8 refer to the following announcement.

Attention: We have just been informed that the expected hurricane will reach our area sometime tonight. Local authorities have declared a weather emergency. Strong winds and very heavy rains are forecast. In fact, as you know, it is raining very heavily right now, and flooding is predicted. We have decided to close the office early today so all employees can return home safely. All employees may leave immediately, but please remember to properly shut down and unplug your computers and electrical equipment. A small group of supervisors and security personnel will remain in the building overnight in case of emergencies. Thank you. (112 words)

7.

Why are some employees staying?
  a. To unplug the electrical equipment.
  b. Only overnight.
  c. In case of emergencies.
  d. Because of flooding.

8.

What should employees do before leaving?
  a. Leave immediately. b. Drive safely.
  c. Close the office early. d. Turn off their computers.

設問 7——8 は以下の告知に関するものです。
　皆様に申し上げます。予報されているハリケーンが今夜当地域にやって来るとの情報を得ました。地元当局は，気象非常事態を宣言しました。強風と非常な豪雨が予報されています。実際，ご承知の通り現在もひどい雨が降っていますし，洪水が予測されています。全従業員が安全に帰宅できるように，本日はオフィスを早く閉めることに決定しました。全従業員は直ちに退社していただけますが，皆さんのコンピュータを正しくシャットダウンし電気設備のプラグを抜くのを忘れないで下さい。監督者と警備要員の小グループが，非常事態に備えて一晩構内に残ります。ありがとうございます。

解答

7.　　　　　　　　　　　　　　　　　　　　　　　　　c

訳 なぜ数人の従業員が残るのですか。
　a. 電気設備の栓を抜くため。　　b. 一泊だけ。
　c. 非常事態にそなえて。　　　　d. 氾濫のため。

　・・・・・・・・・・・・・・・・・・・・・・・・・・・・

参考 文末に監督者と警備要員が非常事態に備えて構内に残るとある。

8.　　　　　　　　　　　　　　　　　　　　　　　　　d

訳 従業員は退社する前に何をするべきですか。
　a. 直ちに去る。　　　　　　　b. 安全運転する。
　c. 早くオフィスを閉める。　　d. 彼らのコンピュータのスイッチを切る。

　・・・・・・・・・・・・・・・・・・・・・・・・・・・・

参考 6行目から7行目にかけて，コンピュータを正しくシャットダウンし電気設備のプラグを抜くのを忘れないようにとの指示がある。

Questions 9 — 11 refer to the following news item.

Prices of 10-year government bond futures fell slightly Thursday due to adjustment selling ahead of the upcoming 3-day weekend. The markets will be closed on Friday for Memorial Day. The price of October futures contracts for 10-year bonds was down .7 of a percentage point from Wednesday to 128.3 sending the yield up 1.45 percentage points. The yield on the new Gold Star 10-year bonds rose .3 of a percentage point to 1.43 percent. (798 words)

9.
What is this story mostly about?
   a. Bond yields.
   b. A feasibility study.
   c. Percentage speculation.
   d. A feature story.

10.
Why will the market be closed?
   a. Because of the political situation.
   b. Because of a national holiday.
   c. Because trading was halted.
   d. Because bond futures fell.

11.
What is the new yield for Gold Star bonds?
   a. 0.7%
   b. 128.3
   c. 1.43%
   d. 0.3%

設問 9 — 11 は，以下のニュースについてのものです。
　10年の国債先物の価格は，木曜日，3日後にやってくる週末を前にして，調整のための売りでわずかに下がりました。市場はメモリアルデーのため金曜日はお休みです。10年債の10月の先物契約価格は，水曜日から0.7％下がり128.3となり利回りは1.45でした。新しいゴールドスター10年債の利回りは，0.3％上昇し1.43パーセントとなりました。

解答

9.   a

訳 この話は大体何についてのものですか。
- a. 債券の利回り。
- b. 採算性の調査。
- c. パーセンテージ投機。
- d. 特集記事。

参考 fell, the yield, down, rose という語群から推測できる事は何かを考える。　futures「先物商品，先物取引」

10.   b

訳 市場はどうして閉まるのですか。
- a. 政状のため。
- b. 祭日のため。
- c. 取引が停止したので。
- d. 先物債券が下落したので。

参考 メモリアルデー（戦没将兵記念日5月最後の月曜日）のため。

11.   c

訳 ゴールドスター債の新利回りは何ですか。
- a. 0.7％
- b. 128.3
- c. 1.43％
- d. 0.3％

参考 文末に1.43パーセントとなったとある。

Questions 12 — 14 refer to the following advertisement.

Ritter and Associates, one of the countries leading investment firms, would like you to consider us for all your financial needs. Not only are we licensed brokers for stocks, bonds, and other types of securities, we also offer financial planning, accounting services, and currency trading advisement. Ritter and Associates have been listed on the New York and other stock exchanges for over 70 years. Our expertise is broad and our track record over the years is very impressive. Just ask any of our satisfied clients. We invite you to inquire about the many ways that we might improve your current financial situation. Our staff of qualified professionals is always available for consultations. In addition to our offices in the United States, we maintain branch offices in every major city in Asia, Europe, and South America. (135 words)

12.
Who can call Ritter and Associates?
    a. Satisfied clients.   b. Consultants.
    c. Professionals.   d. Any individual.

13.
What are Ritter and Associates' primary services?
    a. Securities trading.   b. Accounting.
    c. Loans.   d. Issuing bonds.

14.
Which markets does Ritter not deal in?
    a. Currency.   b. Real estate.
    c. Bonds.   d. Stocks.

設問12 — 14は，以下の広告に関するものです。
　リッター&アソーシエイツは，この国の一流投資企業の一つです。あなたの金融ニーズの全てを私どもにお任せいただきたいと思います。私どもは株，債券その他証券を取扱う公認ブローカーであり，財務計画，会計サービスと通貨取引のアドバイスも提供いたします。リッター&アソーシエイツはニューヨーク及び他の証券取引所で70年余り上場されています。弊社の専門知識は広く，実績は長年にわたり非常に素晴らしいものです。満足されている私どものお客様にお尋ね下さい。あなたの現在の財政状況を改善する多くの方法について問い合わせて下さるようにお勧めします。正規の専門家である私どものスタッフは，常にご相談に応じられます。アメリカ合衆国のオフィスに加え，アジア，ヨーロッパと南アメリカの全主要都市に支社がございます。

解答

12.　　　　　　　　　　　　　　　　　　　　　　　　　　　　　d

訳 リッター&アソーシエイツに電話をかけるのは誰ですか。
　a. 満足した顧客。　　　　b. コンサルタント。
　c. 専門家。　　　　　　　d. 誰でもよい。

参考 当社に金融ニーズを任せてくれと一般大衆に宣伝している。

13.　　　　　　　　　　　　　　　　　　　　　　　　　　　　　a

訳 リッター&アソーシエイツの主要なサービスは何ですか。
　a. 証券取引。　　　　　　b. 会計。
　c. ローン。　　　　　　　d. 債権発行。

参考 3行目に stocks, bonds, and other types of securities とある。

14.　　　　　　　　　　　　　　　　　　　　　　　　　　　　　b

訳 リッターが取引しない市場はどれですか。
　a. 通貨。　　　　　　　　b. 不動産。
　c. 債券。　　　　　　　　d. 株。

参考 advisement「熟考，助言」

Questions 15 — 17 refer to the following report.

As these charts show, I'm happy to announce that the sales staff has surpassed the previous years' sales objective by 17%. This was accomplished by the dedication and efforts of the entire department, from the secretaries to the department head, but especially the field staff, whose assertive efforts and tireless dedication brought about this outstanding achievement. On this occasion I would like to announce that all department members below the managerial level will receive an extra 15% added to their yearly bonuses while all others will receive a comparable amount in stock options. Congratulations.

(93 words)

15.
Why are the employees getting extra bonus money?
    a. Due to the hard work of the entire company.
    b. The president is generous.
    c. All departments contributed equally.
    d. Due to the high sales volume.

16.
Who will get stock options?
    a. Workers who sold over 17%.   b. The entire field staff.
    c. Managers and executives.   d. All white-collar workers.

17.
What happened to last year's sales goal?
    a. It was 15%.
    b. A staff member made assertive efforts.
    c. Its objective was 17% lower.
    d. It was increased by 17%.

設問15 — 17は，以下のレポートに関するものです。
　これらのチャートが示すように，販売スタッフが前年の販売目的を17％超えたと発表できる事をうれしく思います。これは秘書から部長まで部全員の献身と努力によって達成されました，しかし，特に現場のスタッフの，積極的な努力と疲れを知らない献身がこの目覚しい業績をもたらしたのです。この機会に，管理レベルの以下の全部員が年間ボーナスの15％増額を受け，その他の全員がストック・オプションでそれに相当するものを受けると発表したいと思います。おめでとうございます。

|解答|

15.   d

|訳| 従業員はなぜ特別ボーナスをもらっているのですか。
　　a. 社全体の頑張りのため。　　b. 社長は気前がよい。
　　c. 全部門が等しく貢献した。　d. 販売額が多かったため。

|参考| 販売スタッフが前年の販売目的を17％超えた事が発表されている。

16.   c

|訳| ストック・オプションを得るのは誰ですか。
　　a. 17％を販売した労働者。　　b. フィールド・スタッフ全員。
　　c. マネージャーと重役。　　　d. 全てのホワイトカラー労働者。

|参考| stock option　ストック・オプション，社員持ち株制度，自社株購入権（報酬として与えられる。）

17.   d

|訳| 去年の販売目標に対してはどのようなことが起こりましたか。
　　a. それは15％だった。　　　　b. 職員が積極的に努力した。
　　c. その目標は17％低かった。　d. それは17％も増加した。

|参考| assent「～を断言する」も覚えよう

Questions 18 — 20 refer to the following advertisement.

Subscribe now to *Women's Health* magazine for a year and we will include free, the book *Exercising for Your Heart*. Yes, that's right, you get 12 issues of the best women's health magazine ever plus an invaluable free book for only $23.98. And if you subscribe before July 15th we'll also give you an aerobic jazz exercise video as an added free bonus. Payment can be made either by personal check, credit card, or money order. Do not send cash. (80 words)

18.

What do you get if you subscribe before July 15th?
- a. A free book and a video.
- b. 12 issues.
- c. A free book.
- d. An aerobics video.

19.

How should you not pay?
- a. Money order.
- b. Cash.
- c. Credit card.
- d. Check.

20.

How long is the subscription for?
- a. Until July 15th.
- b. Twenty-three weeks.
- c. A year.
- d. Until you cancel.

設問18 — 20は以下の広告に関してのものです。
　今すぐに女性の健康誌に1年間定期購読を申し込んでください，そうなさると「心臓のための運動」という本が無料進呈となります。はい，その通りです，あなたはわずか23.98ドルで最高の女性健康誌12冊と有益な無料進呈本が手に入ります。さらに，もし7月15日より前に応募なさる場合はエアロビックス・ジャズ体操のビデオを無料ボーナスとしてお付けします。支払いは個人小切手でも，クレジットカードでも為替でも可能です。現金は送らないで下さい。

|解答|

18.　　　　　　　　　　　　　　　　　　　　　　　　　　a

訳 7月15日以前に定期購読の申込みをする場合は何がもらえますか。
　a. 無料進呈本とビデオ。　　b. 12冊。（12回分のこと。）
　c. 無料進呈本。　　　　　　d. エアロビックスのビデオ。

参考 invaluable「有益な，計り知れないほど貴重な」

19.　　　　　　　　　　　　　　　　　　　　　　　　　　b

訳 支払いができないのは？
　a. 為替。　　　　　　　　　b. 現金。
　c. クレジットカード。　　　d. 小切手

参考 文末に「現金は送らないように」と述べている。

20.　　　　　　　　　　　　　　　　　　　　　　　　　　c

訳 購読期間はどのくらいですか。
　a. 7月15日まで。　　　　　b. 23週。
　c. 1年。　　　　　　　　　d. あなたが解約するまで。

参考 冒頭でsubscribe for a yearと明言している。

Part IV 説明文問題

Questions 21 — 23 refer to the following talk.

Recently the Florida Chamber of Commerce surveyed several hundred higher level executives, department heads, and office managers to find out what were the most common personnel problems in regards to running a modern office. Surprisingly, 86% responded that personal problems among employees was number one. Others were job dissatisfaction, working environment, lack of confidence in management, and, for a small minority, money. In previous surveys money was ranked much higher. (71 words)

21.

What was the biggest problem?
    a. Problems among workers.   b. Money.
    c. Job dissatisfaction.   d. Running an office.

22.

When was the survey conducted?
    a. Previously.   b. A short time ago.
    c. Eight years ago.   d. In 1986.

23.

How many people were surveyed ?
    a. 86 percent.
    b. Executives and office managers.
    c. Several hundred.
    d. All of the Florida Chamber of Commerce.

設問21 — 23は以下の話に関するものです。
　最近，フロリダ商工会議所は，現代のオフィス運営において最もよくある人事問題が何であるかを知るために数百人もの重役と部長とオフィス・マネージャーを調査しました。驚くべきことに86%の人たちが従業員間の問題が1番であると答えました。他は，仕事上の不満，労働環境，経営陣に対しての信頼の欠如そして，少数派でしたが，金銭もありました。以前の調査においては，金銭のランキングがもっと上でした。

|解答|

21.　　　　　　　　　　　　　　　　　　　　　　　　a

|訳| 最も大きい問題は何でしたか。
　a．労働者間の問題。　　　b．お金。
　c．仕事上の不満。　　　　d．オフィスの運営。

|参考| 86%の人たちが従業員間の問題が1番であると答えたと言っている。

22.　　　　　　　　　　　　　　　　　　　　　　　　b

|訳| 調査はいつ実施されましたか。
　a．以前に。　　　　　　　b．ちょっと前。
　c．8年前。　　　　　　　d．1986年。

|参考| 冒頭で「最近」と述べている。

23.　　　　　　　　　　　　　　　　　　　　　　　　c

|訳| 何人の人々が調査されましたか。
　a．86パーセント。　　　　b．重役とオフィス・マネージャー。
　c．数百。　　　　　　　　d．フロリダ商工会議所の全部。

|参考| 数百人の重役と部長，マネージャーを対象にした調査であったとある。

Part IV　説明文問題　　235

Questions 24 — 26 refer to the following announcement

Excuse me. Make sure all of you have a number. The mechanics will look at your cars on a first-come, first-serve basis. I'd like to ask you all to fill out one of the forms on the table. There are pens there also. Briefly state the nature of your car's problem. Be sure to include the make, model and year so we can expedite things. After you've completed the form, the mechanics will look at your car when your number is called.

(85 words)

24.
Why should the make, model and year be written?
- a. For the dealers.
- b. So the car can be fixed.
- c. To eliminate models.
- d. To make things go faster.

25.
What should customers do first?
- a. Take a number.
- b. State the problem.
- c. Fill out the form.
- d. Take a pen.

26.
Who will be served first?
- a. The one with the newest model.
- b. The one with the lowest number.
- c. Whoever comes to the garage.
- d. The one with the biggest problem.

設問24 — 26は次の告知に関してのものです。
　恐れ入りますが，皆様方全員がナンバーをお持ちか確かめて下さい。整備士はお出でになった順番で車を拝見します。テーブルにある書式の1枚に記入なさるようお願いいたします。ペンもそこにございます。問題点の内容を簡単にお書きください。迅速な処置ができますように，必ず種類，型式と年度を書き入れるように願います。書式に記入が終わられた後，皆さんの番号が呼ばれ，整備士が皆さんのお車を拝見します。

|解答|

24.
d

訳 種類と型と年が記入されなければならないのは何故ですか。
- a. 整備士のために。
- b. 車が修理されるように。
- c. モデルを排除するため。
- d. 事をいっそう速くすすめるため。

参考 expedite「はかどらせる，効率よくする」

25.
a

訳 顧客は最初に何をするべきですか。
- a. ナンバーをもらう。
- b. 問題を述べる。
- c. 書式に記入する。
- d. ペンをとる。

参考 文章の流れを記憶する練習かメモを取ることで対処する。

26.
b

訳 誰が最初に（車を）修理してもらうのですか。
- a. 最新型の車を持った人。
- b. 最も若いナンバーの人。
- c. ガレージに来る人は誰でも。
- d. 最も大きい問題を持っている人。

参考 文末に「皆さんの番号順に車を見る」と言っている。

Questions 27 — 29 refer to the following weather report.

As you know, it's been raining all day and is a little chilly. Unfortunately, this gloomy weather is going to continue for at least another day. However, we have a good forecast for the weekend. By Friday evening, skies should be clearing due to a high pressure front coming in from the west, so Saturday and Sunday will be sunny, with warm temperatures and mild breezes. Winter is just around the corner so enjoy the warm weather while you can. Now, back to the news.   (84 words)

27.
What will happen on Friday?
- a. Winter will start.
- b. The rain will continue.
- c. It will clear up.
- d. It will be gloomy.

28.
What is "just around the corner?"
- a. The news.
- b. A good forecast.
- c. Warm weather.
- d. Winter.

29.
What's the weather like now?
- a. Raining.
- b. High pressure.
- c. A little damp.
- d. Clearing.

設問27 — 29は次の天気予報に関するものです。
　皆さんご存知のように一日中雨が降っており，少々寒いです。残念なことに，うっとうしい天気は少なくとももう一日の間続きます。しかし，週末の予報は良いものです。金曜日の晩までに雲が消え，西から高気圧前線が張り出すため土曜と日曜は晴れて暖かくなり，穏やかな風が吹くでしょう。冬がそこまで来ていますから，暖かい天気を楽しめる時に楽しんでおきましょう。では，ニュースに戻ります。

|解答|

27.　　　　　　　　　　　　　　　　　　　　　　c
訳 金曜日には何が起こるのですか。
　　a. 冬が始まる。　　　　　　　b. 雨が続く。
　　c. 晴れる。　　　　　　　　　d. うっとうしくなる。

参考 3行目から4行目にかけて「金曜日の晩までに雲が消える」とある。

28.　　　　　　　　　　　　　　　　　　　　　　d
訳 何が「そこまで来ている」のですか。
　　a. ニュース。　　　　　　　　b. 良い予報。
　　c. 暖い天候。　　　　　　　　d. 冬。

参考 文末に "Winter is just around the corner." とある。

29.　　　　　　　　　　　　　　　　　　　　　　a
訳 現在の天気はどうですか。
　　a. 雨が降っている。　　　　　b. 高気圧。
　　c. 少しジメジメしている。　　d. クリアになること。

参考 冒頭で "it's been raining all day..." と言っている。

Questions 30 — 33 refer to the following advertisement.

Traveling to Sydney on business? On your next trip we would like you to consider the Heritage House Hotel. We are located ideally, only five minutes from the downtown business and financial areas. We have special rates for business people staying more than three nights and paying with a company credit card. We offer both single and double occupancy, and connecting rooms can be arranged. Rates include the breakfast of your choice, a free limousine to and from the airport, and access to all hotel facilities at no extra charge. These include pool, gym, meeting rooms, and a complete business center. The business center is fully equipped with private cubicles, computers, fax machines, copiers, and personal secretaries if needed. We hope to see you soon. (120 words)

30.
What do the rates not include?
- a. Breakfast.
- b. Meeting rooms.
- c. Limousine service.
- d. Valet parking.

31.
What is a good reason for a businessman to stay at this hotel?
- a. Sydney is a beautiful city.
- b. Breakfast is free.
- c. Its proximity to the financial section.
- d. A reasonable charge for the sports facilities.

32.
How can you get the best rates?
- a. Pay by company voucher.
- b. Stay for only one day.
- c. Stay in connecting rooms.
- d. Use a company credit card.

33.
Who would probably not stay here?
- a. Honeymooners.
- b. Executives.
- c. Salespeople.
- d. Managers.

設問30 — 33は次の広告に関するものです。

仕事でシドニーに旅をするのですか。あなたの次のご旅行には私どものヘリテッジ・ハウス・ホテル をご考慮願いたいと思います。当ホテルはダウンタウンのビジネスと金融地区からのほんの5分という理想的な場所に位置しております。3泊以上のご滞在で，会社クレジットカードで支払いを行われるビジネス関係の方々には特別料金がございます。お一人での使用，お二人での使用の提供，そして，接続部屋も手配可能です。料金は，お好きな朝食，リムジンによる空港往復の無料送迎とホテルの全設備へのアクセスを含んでおります。これらは，プール，ジム，会議室と全てが揃ったビジネス・センターを含みます。ご必要ならば，ビジネス・センターには個人用オフィス，コンピュータ，ファックス，複写機と個人用の秘書の全てが揃っております。すぐにお目にかかれることを願っております。

解答

30. **d**
訳 料金に含まれていないものは何ですか。
 a. 朝食。 b. 会議室。
 c. リムジン・サービス。 d. 係員つき駐車サービス。

参考 朝食，無料送迎とホテルの全設備へのアクセスを含むがdの事項はない。

31. **c**
訳 ビジネスマンがこのホテルに泊まる正当な理由は何ですか。
 a. シドニーは美しい都市です。 b. 朝食が無料。
 c. 金融地区へ近接している。 d. スポーツ設備使用料が手ごろ。

参考 特別料金，ロケーション，設備などがホテル選択の理由になりうる。

32. **d**
訳 どうすれば一番手ごろな料金にできますか。
 a. 会社のバウチャーで支払う。 b. 一日だけ泊る。
 c. 接続した部屋に泊る。 d. 会社クレジットカードを使う。

参考 voucher とは旅行業者が旅行者に渡すクーポン券

33. **a**
訳 ここに滞在しないような人はどういう人ですか。
 a. 新婚旅行者。 b. 重役。
 c. 販売員。 d. マネージャー。

参考 選択肢から判断してもaが当てはまらないことがわかる。

Questions 34 — 36 refer to the following presentation.

Let me welcome you all today to this presentation on restaurant service and catering. I would like to talk to you about some topics concerning our industry today.

First, I will discuss those qualities essential for restaurant managers; second, those qualities desirable in a waiter or waitress; and finally, those qualities essential for both. A restaurant manager needs to be very well organized, able to motivate other staff members, and to be imaginative and creative. A waiter or waitress should always be good at dealing with different kinds of people, have good manners, and be able to work as part of a team. Those qualities common both to managers and serving staff are tactfulness, charm, cleanliness, and good health. I will go into more detail on the specific characteristics after lunch, during the second half of the presentation. Remember, whether you are a manager or a server, you should consider yourselves food service professionals at all times. (147 words)

34.
What is the main topic of the presentation?
- a. Hotel management.
- b. Banquet arrangements.
- c. A luncheon meeting.
- d. Restaurant service.

35.
What should servers regard themselves as at all times?
- a. Employees.
- b. Managers.
- c. Professionals.
- d. Charming.

36.
Who is the speaker at this presentation?
- a. A waitress.
- b. A chef.
- c. A caterer.
- d. None of these.

設問34から36は，次のプレゼンテーションに関するものです。
　本日はレストラン・サービスと仕出しサービスについての当プレゼンテーションにようこそお越しくださいました。今日の我々の産業に関して，いくつかのトピックをお話したいと思います。第一はレストランの支配人にとって不可欠な資質，第二はウェイターまたはウェイトレスにとって望まれる資質です。そして最後が，その両方にとって不可欠な資質についてです。レストランの支配人は非常に能率的で，他のスタッフ・メンバーに動機を与えて，想像力に富み，創造的なことができることが必要です。ウェイターまたはウェイトレスは，常にいろいろな種類の人々を扱うのが得意でなければならず，マナーも良く，チームの一員として働けなければなりません。支配人と給仕スタッフに共通する資質は，機転，魅力，清潔と健康です。昼食後は，特徴について具体的にプレゼンテーションの後半でもっと詳しくお話しいたします。皆さんは支配人であれ，給仕であれ，ご自分を食物サービス専門家とみなさなければならないことを覚えておいてください。

解答

34.   d

訳 このプレゼンテーションの主題は何ですか。
　　a. ホテルの経営。　　　　b. 宴会の用意。
　　c. 昼食会。　　　　　　　d. レストランのサービス。

参考 冒頭で「レストラン・サービスと仕出しサービス」と述べられている。

35.   c

訳 給仕達は自分達が何であると思うべきですか。
　　a. 従業員。　　　　　　　b. 支配人。
　　c. 専門家。　　　　　　　d. 魅力的。

参考 文末に「自分を食物サービス専門家とみなすように」と述べている。

36.   d

訳 このプレゼンテーションのスピーカーは誰ですか。
　　a. ウェイトレス。　　　　b. コック長。
　　c. 宴会業者。　　　　　　d. これらのどれもない。

参考 支配人やその他の人々を奨励できる立場の人がスピーカーである。
　　　caterer: 宴会業者の他に「料理の仕出屋」「サービス係」の意味もある。

Questions 37 — 40 refer to the following memo.

Effective June 1st, 20 new fully-automated robot assembly machines will be put into operation in our production plant on a 24-hour basis. After several feasibility studies, it has been determined that these machines will make our production operations much more effective in both terms of cost and efficiency. These machines will replace approximately 400 employees. However there is no need for alarm. There will be no layoffs. The company will gradually reduce the number of employees through natural attrition, early retirement bonuses, retraining, and a moratorium on the hiring of new employees for three years. Management encourages all employees to discuss these restructuring ideas with their supervisors to see what the best course for each individual would be. Thank you.   (120 words)

37.
What can be said about the 400 employees?
- a. They will all be retrained. b. They will not lose their jobs.
- c. They need to be alarmed. d. No one will be hired.

38.
Why were the new machines installed?
- a. Because they are more cost effective.
- b. Due to the moratorium.
- c. So that they can operate on a limited basis.
- d. Because of the new project.

39.
When will the company hire new employees?
- a. When they run efficiently.   b. Next June.
- c. When they are fully trained.   d. After a few years.

40.
What are current employees encouraged to do?
- a. Get advice from their supervisors.
- b. Resign at once to get a bonus.
- c. Look for a new job.
- d. Get training to operate the robots.

設問37から40は次のメモに関するものです。

6月1日から、新しい全自動組立てロボット20機が、24時間体制で当社生産工場での運転を開始します。いくつかの企業化調査の後、これらの機械がコスト面および効率面で当社の生産作業により大きい効果をもたらすことがわかりました。これらの機械は約400人の従業員にとって替わります。しかし、心配はいりません、一時解雇はありません。会社は自然な人員削減、早期引退ボーナス、再訓練及び3年間の新入社員雇用停止を行い、徐々にこれらの従業員を削減します。経営層はこれらリストラのアイデアについて全従業員が各々のスーパーバイザーと話し合い、各々に一番良い進路が何であるかを決めるように奨励します。ありがとう。

解答

37. b
[訳] 400人の従業員についてどんな事が言えますか。
- a. 全員が再訓練される。
- b. 失業しない。
- c. 懸念する必要がある。
- d. 誰も雇用されない。

[参考] 6行目にレイオフ（解雇）はないと述べられている。

38. a
[訳] 新しい機械が設置されたのはなぜですか。
- a. それらの費用有効性が一層大きいから。
- b. 支払猶予期間によって。
- c. 限られた体制で操業できるように。
- d. 新プロジェクトのために。

[参考] 「コストと効率面で大きい効果をもたらす」（4～5行目）とある。

39. d
[訳] 会社が新入社員を雇うのはいつですか。
- a. それらが効率的に可動するとき。
- b. 次の6月。
- c. 彼らが充分に訓練された時。
- d. 2～3年後。

[参考] aやcの事項については言及されていない。

40. a
[訳] 現在の従業員はどうするように奨励されていますか。
- a. 彼らの監督者からアドバイスを得る。
- b. すぐ辞職しボーナスをもらう。
- c. 新しい仕事を捜す。
- d. ロボット操作の訓練を受ける。

[参考] 文末に「スーパーバイザーと話し合い進路を決めるように」とある。

TOEIC®テスト リスニング・パート攻略　　CD付き

2003年 5月 20日　　1刷
2006年 6月 14日　　2刷
著　者 ── 柴田バネッサ／ロバート・ウェスト
　　　　　　©Shibata Vanessa / Robert West, 2003

発行者 ── 南雲　一範
発行所 ── 株式会社　南雲堂
　　　　　東京都新宿区山吹町361（〒162-0801）
　　　　　電話　　03-3268-2384（営業部）
　　　　　　　　　03-3268-2387（編集部）
　　　　　FAX　　03-3260-5425（営業部）
　　　　　振替口座：00160-0-46863
印刷所／木元省美堂　　製本所／笠原製本　　DTP／アサイトキコ

　　　　E-mail　nanundo@post.email.ne.jp（編集部）
　　　　URL　　http://www.nanun-do.co.jp
　　　　Printed in Japan　　〈検印省略〉

乱丁、落丁本はご面倒ですが小社通販係宛ご送付下さい。送料小社負担にてお取り替えいたします。

ISBN 4-523-26410-4　C0082〈1-410〉

CD付

TOEICテスト英文法攻略

柴田バネッサ
ロバート・ウェスト

A5判　定価（本体1,900円＋税）

- ◆ スコアアップに即効のある重要着眼点170を掲載。
- ◆ TOEICのPartⅤ & PartⅥの文法、語彙問題を中心に頻出問題の傾向と対策を検討。
- ◆ 出題頻度の高いものを知ることにより、タイムロスと失点を防止。
- ◆ 文法を基礎からチェックしたい人、一気に点数アップを狙う人のために全パターンをカバーする340題を用意。
- ◆ TOEIC用語300を効率的に覚える頻出語リストを用意した。

南雲堂